MW01265209

Your Kind of Power

A HISTORY OF THE

GUADALUPE VALLEY
ELECTRIC COOPERATIVE
1938–2013

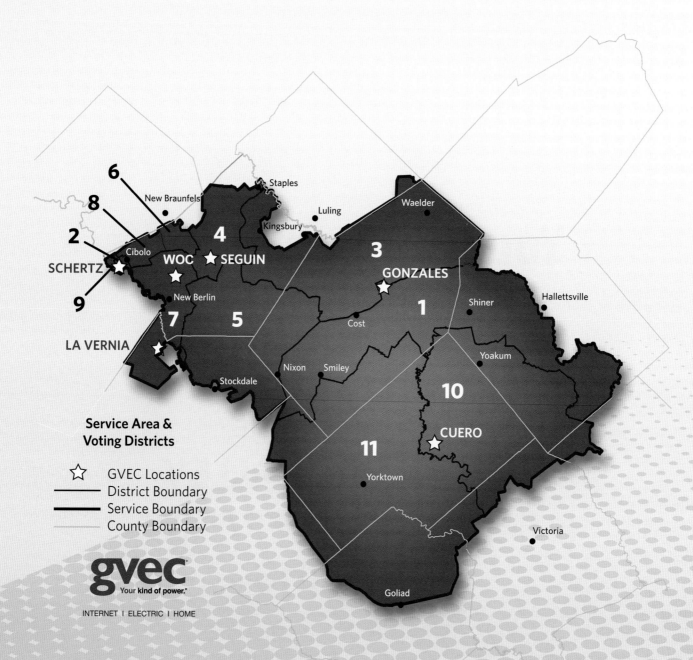

6

8

2

SCHERTZ

9

LA VERNIA

New Braunfels

Staples

Cibolo

WOC

4

SEGUIN

New Berlin

7

5

Stockdale

Kingsbury

Luling

Waelder

3

GONZALES

Cost

Nixon

Smiley

1

Shiner

Hallettsville

Yoakum

10

CUERO

11

Yorktown

Goliad

Victoria

**Service Area &
Voting Districts**

☆   GVEC Locations
——   District Boundary
━━   Service Boundary
——   County Boundary

gvec
Your kind of power.*

INTERNET | ELECTRIC | HOME

THE
DONNING COMPANY
PUBLISHERS

Your Kind of Power

A HISTORY OF THE
GUADALUPE VALLEY
ELECTRIC COOPERATIVE
1938–2013

by Tammy Thompson
and Bill Beck

The Donning Company Publishers
184 Business Park Drive, Suite 206
Virginia Beach, VA 23462

Lex Cavanah, General Manager
Nathan Stufflebean, Donning Production Supervisor
Richard A. Horwege, Senior Editor
Jeremy Glanville, Graphic Designer
Monika Ebertz, Imaging Artist
Kathy Snowden Railey, Project Research Coordinator
Katie Gardner, Marketing and Production Coordinator

James H. Railey, Project Director

Library of Congress Cataloging-in-Publication Data

Names: Thompson, Tammy, author. | Beck, Bill, author.
Title: Your kind of power : a history of the Guadalupe Valley Electric
    Cooperative, 1938–2013 / by Tammy Thompson and Bill Beck.
Description: Virginia Beach, VA : Donning Company Publishers, [2016] |
    Includes bibliographical references and index.
Identifiers: LCCN 2016024530 | ISBN 9781681840574 (hard cover : alk. paper)
Subjects: LCSH: Guadalupe Valley Electric Cooperative. | Electric
    cooperatives—Texas—History. | Electric utilities—Texas—History.
Classification: LCC HD9688.U54 G884 2016 | DDC 334/.68133379320976425—
    dc23
LC record available at https://lccn.loc.gov/2016024530

Printed in the United States of America at Walsworth

Table of Contents

Celebrating

75

YEARS

A Message from the
Board President and General Manager

Today, one is hard-pressed to find a cooperative member who recalls the "good old days" when the lights first came on. Electricity added a new dimension to rural life that made it easier, more productive. Folks were excited about their Cooperative. They knew the joy of the first light bulb, the benefits of the first electric stove, and the convenience electric motors brought to the farm. It was a loyalty like no other and a precious aspect of cooperative ownership.

Fast forward seventy-five years where the world and the Cooperative look very different. We've grown exponentially from that first 150 meters served in 1940. The majority of us are second-generation GVEC members who have always had electricity readily available—as it should be with today's technologies. We've formed an expectation that the lights will be on when we need them. That generational change has caused GVEC to progressively engage in services that redefine the value you can, and should, expect from your Cooperative.

GVEC celebrated seventy-five years of service to the membership in December 2013. This was an important opportunity to look back on the small group of farmers and ranchers in the Monthalia-Bebe area (near Gonzales) who set their sights on a better life. Little did they know, their efforts would set a standard of service that remains steadfast as our strategies and goals evolve with the changing needs of our membership.

It's a good feeling to reflect on the passion and determination the folks had in the beginning: all to give their members more. It reminds us that our core values of striving to exceed your needs and caring for our communities reflect our greater responsibility to deliver more than electricity.

This seventy-five-year historical journey of GVEC is dedicated to our pioneering leaders who came before us, those employees who have served and proudly stand with us today, and members past and present who give us our purpose.

Serving your needs is more than just a job to us. It is a commitment we have made to add value to your life, family, and community. We are sincerely proud and privileged to serve you.

Respectfully,

Lewis Borgfeld
Board President

Darren Schauer
General Manager and CEO

Preface

Dedicated to the past and present members and employees of the Guadalupe Valley Electric Cooperative, this book celebrates seventy-five years of milestones and the good people that have made them possible. This is the story of GVEC featuring a few personal glimpses into who, why, and how we serve. To all involved over the years, we humbly extend our sincere appreciation for your support and important contributions to our accomplishments and growth.

Our Cooperative history is written by topic as opposed to date. Each chapter will give you a sense of changes and experiences in the specific areas that have shaped GVEC into who we are today. This may be an unconventional way to present history for some, but through the reading you will find that GVEC is a leader in taking the untraditional path when it makes sense. However, experience has taught us you must be flexible to meet the needs of a diverse audience. Therefore, a chronological timeline has also been included for those who prefer a more direct approach to our story.

We invite you to make this reading your own memorable experience. Reminisce about your life experiences in the Guadalupe Valley and the changes you've seen. Do you recognize former coworkers? Did you ever use some of the equipment mentioned or know someone who worked at CMC Steel when it was originally SMI? Perhaps a photo jogs memories of your grandma's old heater or you learned to cook on a brand-new appliance in school. If you have lived, worked, or played in the Guadalupe Valley between 1938 and 2013, chances are you have a connection to GVEC. We think you'll be pleasantly surprised at just how many unexpected ways GVEC has empowered the lives and communities it has served for seventy-five years—and counting.

In 1946, the Board of Directors approved moving the headquarters office to Gonzales on Saint Paul Street.

Chapter One

A Rich HERITAGE

The early years of bringing electricity to rural areas were riddled with challenges, yet worth the effort for the life-changing benefits electricity would bring to farm life. The Guadalupe Valley Electric Cooperative established a strong foundation during this time that would set the stage for the next seventy-five years of leadership and service to its industry, members, and communities.

By the mid-1930s, electric power was a reality in Texas, as well as much of the United States. But much of the rural areas still could not enjoy one of the world's greatest inventions. Decades earlier in 1879, Thomas Edison had demonstrated the feasibility of incandescent lighting at his West Orange, New Jersey laboratories, and four years later, had made Pearl Street Station in Lower Manhattan the first integrated electric generation, transmission, and distribution system.

Inspired by personal experience in a small Georgia town lacking access to electricity, President Franklin Delano Roosevelt led the charge for rural electrification by helping to fund and develop electric cooperatives. *Photo courtesy of FDR Library Online*

During the next half-century, electric power created a new industrial and economic revolution in American society. Electricity lighted homes and offices, created new labor-saving appliances, powered factories, and electric street railways shortened travel times for millions of urban Americans.

But even more millions of Americans were completely shut out from the revolutionary changes that electricity was bringing to society. Throughout the latter years of the nineteenth century and the first two decades of the twentieth century, electrification was solely an urban phenomenon. In the early 1930s, rural Americans lived much like their ancestors had a hundred years before.

Texas was typical of the trend. In 1935, only about one-third of the state's residents had access to electric power; in sparsely populated rural areas such as South Central Texas, fewer than 5 percent of the residents enjoyed access to electricity. Residents of Dallas, Fort Worth, Houston, San Antonio, Corpus Christi, and other larger Texas cities had electric power; rural residents of the Lone Star State did not.

Starting with the cooperation of farmers just like this one in 1938, the services provided by the Guadalupe Valley Electric Cooperative would enhance the quality of life in rural communities for generations to come. *Photo courtesy of FDR Library Online*

A FEW TYPICAL USES OF ELECTRICITY

IN THE FARM HOME

LIGHTING — RADIO — REFRIGERATION — WASHER — RUNNING WATER — VACUUM CLEANER

ON THE FARM

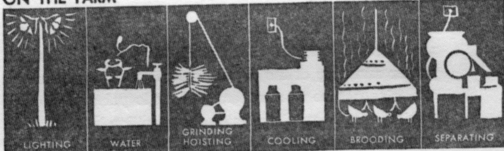

LIGHTING — WATER — GRINDING HOISTING — COOLING — BROODING — SEPARATING

IN THE RURAL SCHOOLS

LIGHTING — HOME ECONOMICS — MOTION PICTURES — RADIO — FARM MECHANICS — SANITATION

FOR RURAL INDUSTRIES

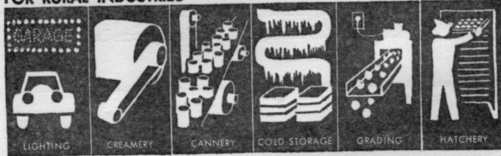

LIGHTING — CREAMERY — CANNERY — COLD STORAGE — GRADING — HATCHERY

PICTORIAL STATISTICS, INC

As a new concept to rural families, education on the value of electricity was important. The newly created Rural Electrification Administration developed posters and other materials to promote interest in using electricity.

That would change with the election of Franklin Delano Roosevelt as president of the United States in 1932. Roosevelt, a rich landowner from Upstate New York and the Empire State's governor, was a polio victim since the 1920s. One of the few places he could gain relief from his condition was the town of Warm Springs in rural Georgia. FDR was appalled that residents of the tiny Georgia community had little access to electric power—and what was available was provided at extortionate rates by an investor-owned utility.

In his 1932 run for the White House, Roosevelt campaigned against the business policies of savvy entrepreneur Samuel Insull of Chicago Edison and the Public Utility Holding Companies, promising those who voted for him that things would change. Once in office, FDR seized the chance to combat the Great Depression with federally funded programs that would provide both jobs and economic betterment to much of rural America. In 1935, Roosevelt unveiled the Tennessee Valley Authority (TVA) and the Rural Electrification Administration (REA). Both programs used electric power to effect huge changes in rural America. TVA built a series of hydroelectric dams on the Tennessee River that provided industrial electric power to modernize an entire farming region of the United States that had been mired in poverty since the end of the Civil War.

The REA created a program of farmer-owned cooperatives that could borrow money from the federal government at low interest rates to build electric distribution lines that would serve rural Americans from coast to coast. Future President Lyndon B. Johnson, then the congressman from the Texas 10th District, and future Speaker of the House of Representatives Sam Rayburn were strong proponents of rural electrification in Texas in the mid- to late 1930s. Their encouragement of rural electrification, coupled with the strong support of the Texas State Grange, an advocacy group for a better life for farmers, helped bring electric power to the state from 1936 to the early 1940s. Texans were early and enthusiastic supporters of the rural electrification concept because life on a Texas farm or ranch in the early 1930s was characterized by backbreaking labor.

The Cooperative Dream Takes Shape

Some that lived in rural areas, like the Lindemann family featured on page 14, used a Delco Plant battery system which gave them enough energy to run things like lighting and radios. Though the portable system lit up their homes at night, it did not provide the fully electrified life that was taking shape across America. Milton D. Lindemann and other rural residents closely followed the activities of the REA and the Texas State Grange concerning rural electrification. He and representatives from local communities in the Gonzales area met in Cost on October 14, 1938, to discuss creating a cooperative that would borrow money from the REA to build one hundred miles of electric distribution line in Gonzales County. The group hired John A. Romberg, a Gonzales attorney, to draw up the papers for the establishment of the Cooperative, and V. L. Beavers, a Victoria-based engineer. Beavers' job was to draw up plans to begin serving Gonzales County families with rural power.[4]

GVEC Is Born

Matters moved quickly from there. In November 1938, representatives of the Texas State Grange from nearby Bexar County began meeting with the Gonzales group, and on December 2, 1938, incorporators formally organized the Guadalupe Valley Electric Cooperative (GVEC) at a meeting in Cost. Nine of the founding members were selected to form the original Board of Directors. Lindemann was chosen president, R. B. Williams of Nixon was named vice president, and H. C. Gillette of Wrightsboro was selected to serve as secretary-treasurer.[5] Other founding directors included Theodore Siepmann of Monthalia, George W. Turk of Dreyer, Charles C. Deschner of Bebe, J. C. Pruett of Schoolland, and Arthur H. Boening and Emil C. Prochnow, both of Converse.[6] Many of the directors were related by marriage, or longtime friends; Siepmann was Lindemann's brother-in-law.

ARTICLES OF INCORPORATION

OF

GUADALUPE VALLEY ELECTRIC COOPERATIVE, INC.

KNOW ALL MEN BY THESE PRESENTS:

We, the undersigned, being natural persons of the age of
twenty-one years or more and citizens and residents of the
State of Texas, for the purpose of forming a corporation under
the "Electric Cooperative Corporation Act" of the State of
Texas, do hereby adopt the following articles of incorporation:

ARTICLE I

The name of the Corporation is

GUADALUPE VALLEY ELECTRIC COOPERATIVE, INC.

ARTICLE II

The purpose or purposes for which the Corporation is organized are to engage in rural electrification and

1- to generate, manufacture, purchase, acquire and accumu-
late electric energy and to transmit, distribute, furnish, sell and dispose of such electric energy to its
members only;

2- to assist its members only to wire their premises and
install therein, and to acquire and supply, electrical
and plumbing appliances, fixtures, machinery, supplies,
apparatus and equiptment of any and all kinds and
character.

ARTICLE III

The name and addresses of the incorporators who shall
serve as directors and manage the affairs of the Corporation
until the first annual meeting of the members or until their
successors are elected and qualified are as follows:

Name:	Address:
M. D. Lindemann	Cost, Texas.
R. B. Williams	Nixon, Texas.
H. C. Gillette	Wrightsboro, Texas.
Chas. C. Deschner	Bebe, Texas.
Geroge W. Turk	Dryer, Texas.
Theodore Siepmann	Monthalia, Texas.
J. C. Pruitt	Smiley, Texas, R.F.D.
Arthur Boenig	Converse, Texas
Emil G. Prochnow	Converse, Texas

The Articles of Incorporation was signed on December 2, 1938, formally establishing the Guadalupe Valley
Electric Cooperative along with a nine-member Board of Directors.

Lindemann's selection as first president of the Cooperative was no surprise. His son, Buster Lindemann, recalled with fond memories that "Daddy had a lot of friends. He knew a lot of people. He was a good organizer. People liked him. People trusted him."[7]

The first order of business for the new Cooperative involved establishing fees. Membership was open to any person or firm in the area who agreed to pay the $5 membership fee and to purchase electric power from GVEC. That $5 was a significant amount of money in rural Texas in the waning days of the Great Depression, and Lindemann and the other directors spent considerable time in the spring of 1939 crisscrossing the county on horseback to sign up new members.

Pioneering Leaders

Milton Lindemann was the first of a succession of competent members who gave their time and talents to GVEC. Selected as the first chairman of the Cooperative's Board of Directors, Lindemann served on the Board for fifteen years and was a strong supporter of the 1941 Board decision to divide the service area into districts, electing one member of the Board from each district and ensuring that control of the Cooperative was not vested in the most populous areas of GVEC.

E. A. Hassman oversaw construction of GVEC's first sections of distribution line and moved on to serve as the first general manager from 1944 to 1952.

The district plan also gave voice in the Cooperative to as many members as possible, even those living in the more isolated areas. Following these new boundaries, yearly district meetings were implemented into the Bylaws of GVEC.

The first GVEC headquarters office was located in the small community of Cost, Texas, just outside Gonzales.

The existing headquarters building on East Sarah DeWitt Drive in Gonzales was opened in June 1965.

Lindemann also provided the key vote in one of the more contentious decisions ever faced by a GVEC Board. In 1946, the REA suggested strongly that the Cooperative's headquarters located at the intersection of Farm to Market Road 466 (FM 466) and State Highway 97 West in Cost was unsuitable because of space limitations and its location was not near a major transportation route. The REA since 1939 had been urging the GVEC Board to locate its headquarters in the nearby community of Gonzales. When the matter did come to a vote in 1946, it was a 4–4 tie. Lindemann, as chairman and a resident of Cost, cast the deciding vote to move the Cooperative's headquarters to Gonzales, where REA quickly approved a loan to purchase and rehabilitate a building at 928 Saint Paul Street that would serve as GVEC headquarters until a new facility was opened at 825 East Sarah DeWitt Drive on June 1, 1965.[8]

Another early order of business involved the hiring of E. A. Hassman as project coordinator for the new Cooperative. Hassman, an electrical worker with practical experience in the field, was originally hired at GVEC about the same time the Cooperative had its first loan approved in April 1939. In 1944, his title and position changed to general manager where he oversaw construction of the A and B Sections of the Cooperative's lines. Hassman served as the first general manager of GVEC until his death in 1952, and was responsible for much of GVEC's early growth.[9] He understood well the benefits associated with electricity and wholeheartedly believed in the value it offered the rough rural farm life.

Milton D. Lindemann served as the first chairman of the Board of Directors from 1938 to 1945 where he led the decision to establish member voting districts and yearly district meetings among other important Cooperative firsts.

District meetings gave members a forum to nominate district directors to represent them and have their voice heard in the business matters of GVEC.

Little did they know, the pioneering efforts of the GVEC founders, neighbors, and politicians would forever change farming operations in the area.

A Moment in Time: Life Without Electricity

There is a chapter in the first volume of Robert Caro's biography of Lyndon Baines Johnson, who was highly involved in the establishment of rural electric cooperatives, entitled "The Sad Irons." The chapter tells the struggle of farm families in Central Texas in the days before rural electrification. The title refers to the practice of heating three or four irons on a wood-fired stove to iron the family clothes on washday.[10]

Robert Meischen and his wife, charter members of DeWitt County Electric Cooperative, which would merge later with GVEC, lived the sad irons on their Yorktown ranch for the first eight years they were married. Meischen, who sadly passed away in October 2013 on his one-hundredth birthday, grew up on a ranch outside Yorktown and attended one of the founding meetings of DeWitt County Electric Cooperative in 1938. The son of German immigrants, Meischen's heritage was still evident at the age of ninety-nine in his slight accent; he did not learn English until he enrolled in primary school. In 1938, Meischen signed the family up for cooperative membership over his mother's objections about the $2.50 cost.

The next year, Meischen and his wife started married life on a two-hundred-acre spread six miles down a gravel road from Yorktown. They raised a little cotton, a little corn, and ran Hereford cattle on the spread. DeWitt County Electric Cooperative promised to extend the lines past their farm in 1939 or 1940, but World War II and its restrictions on civilian use of copper and steel halted rural electrification efforts all over the nation.

It would be 1946 before the Cooperative was able to extend its lines down what is today called the Meischen Road.

Those seven years would mirror what many Texas families experienced before the advent of rural electrification. The Meischens cooked on a wood-fired stove in the kitchen; bread and pastries were kept warm in a warming box in the oven. Meischen recalled he bought a used icebox in San Antonio for $5; he had to make a pan to catch the melting water. The young family had a washboard and wringer to wash clothes. They would heat water in an iron kettle outside to fill the washtub. The dryer was a wire strung between the cookhouse outside and the main house. The young couple had three of the ten-pound sad irons: one in use, one hot on the stove, and one warming up. Meischen said his mother taught him to use an iron when he started attending school dances in the early 1930s.[11]

There was a meat locker in Yorktown that was associated with the community ice plant. Meischen and other area ranchers would rent space in the locker for beef, pork, and venison. When they wanted a roast or meat for the table, they would drive to town to pick up what they needed.

The Rural Electrification Administration (REA) was quick to recognize this fact of postwar life when it began releasing loans and encouraging existing cooperatives to begin building out distribution systems almost as soon as the war was over. The decade after 1946 was one of the most active in REA's history. And candidly, much of the postwar demand for electric service in rural areas of Texas came from the farm wife. Appliances had become commonplace, more affordable and increasingly convenient. Farm wives on the GVEC system wanted access to electric refrigerators, toasters, water heaters, washing machines and dozens of other laborsaving devices.

Acquisition and Building

GVEC accomplished its early growth by acquiring lines through purchase and by building new lines to bring electric power to everyone who wanted it in Guadalupe, Gonzales, Wilson, and Lavaca Counties. During World War II, GVEC began negotiating with City Public Service of San Antonio, which had municipalized San Antonio Public Service Company in 1942, for the transfer of rural lines in Guadalupe County operated by City Public Service. Negotiations dragged on for five years, and in April 1948, GVEC

Established in the Gonzales area, GVEC planted its western service area roots through a 1948 negotiation with City Public Service of San Antonio. In exchange for Cooperative lines near Bexar County, GVEC acquired more than two hundred miles of line in Guadalupe County and a small office and warehouse located on South River Street in Seguin near the Guadalupe County Courthouse. This became the first GVEC office located in the western service area.

The expansion of GVEC members through acquisitions across the service territory meant more lines to build and maintain. Crews, materials, and equipment expanded steadily in the field to keep up with the demands of new growth.

By the 1950s, technology advances in line-building equipment had taken shape and were widespread in the electric utility industry. The use of hydraulics made it possible for line crews to be more productive than ever before in building and maintaining a strong and reliable electric distribution system to withstand many more years of membership growth.

In the early days of electricity, it was not uncommon for rural folks to be hesitant of implementing electricity into their lives. Fearing it was a dangerous and expensive prospect, cooperatives had the chore of education on the use and value of electricity. Shown in the photo, Robert Meischen—featured on page 20, reminisces about his first co-op experience with longtime GVEC employee Wayne Hillman.

acquired sixteen hundred consumers served by more than two hundred miles of line formerly owned by City Public Service. In exchange, GVEC gave up several small rural lines it owned in Bexar County, just outside San Antonio. The 1948 agreement with City Public Service gave the Cooperative distribution lines serving the rural communities of Cibolo, Fentress, Geronimo, Kingsbury, McQueeney, Marion, Prairie Lea, Schertz, Schumannsville, Zuehl, and Zorn. The purchase also included an office and small warehouse in Seguin located on South River Street near the Guadalupe County Courthouse.[22]

In years to come, the acquisition of the City Public Service rural lines would come to have immense significance to GVEC's future growth, as many of the rural communities involved would become the economic engine driving much of the growth in the Cooperative's service territory. In 1949, the Cooperative acquired from Central Power & Light the small distribution system in Cost that had been at the heart of GVEC's formation ten years before.[23]

In the late 1940s and throughout the 1950s, cooperative crews set about expanding GVEC's distribution system to bring low-cost power to new members. Building distribution lines at the time involved surveying and clearing rights-of-way, digging holes to erect power poles, and stringing copper. It was hard work, performed in every kind of weather working with primitive tools and line trucks.

Along with establishing members and lines, securing a reliable power supply was also a critical mission in the early years of GVEC. Washington politicians such as Senator Ralph Yarborough (shown second from left at an REA dinner in 1965) and Congressman J. P. Buchanan supported the establishment of the Lower Colorado River Authority (LCRA) and the resulting completion of the Buchanan Hydroelectric Dam. LCRA became the wholesale power provider to the municipalities and co-ops in a sixteen-county region of South Central Texas. GVEC was among the first customers of LCRA and would remain so for the next seventy-plus years.

By the early to mid-1950s, technological advances stemming from World War II and the Korean War had immense implications for the electric utility industry, especially when it came to line work. Hydraulic and power-takeoff (PTO) technology had been perfected during the war and were widespread in the industry. The conversion of A-frame boom trucks to hydraulically operated boom trucks forever transformed the way, and speed, in which line work was performed.

Securing a Reliable Power Supply

One of the most significant tasks facing GVEC and other rural electric cooperatives in Texas, after recruiting members and building lines, was securing a reliable power supply. In July 1934, Texas Congressman J. P. Buchanan and Texas attorney A. J. Wirtz toured the unfinished Hamilton Dam on the Colorado. Started by a private utility in 1932, the half-finished dam had been shut down in the early days of the Great Depression. Buchanan and Wirtz resolved to do what needed to be done to finish the dam. Buchanan had requested President Roosevelt to fund the completion of the dam by a private company, controlled by Wirtz, and the president replied he would order the Public Works Administration (PWA) to fund the project on one condition: FDR wanted it controlled by a public agency.

Wirtz and Buchanan went to work with the Texas Legislature, which had agreed to establish the Lower Colorado River Authority (LCRA) during a special session in October 1934.[24] With the support of Washington politicians such as Buchanan (who died

The energized lifestyle made possible by GVEC was a convenience rural farm life had never before experienced.

of a heart attack in 1937), Ralph Yarborough, and Lyndon Johnson, the Buchanan Dam was finished in 1938 and began looking for customers in a sixteen-county region of South Central Texas.[25]

PWA loaned the LCRA $5 million to buy out the electrical system of Texas Power & Light in the region, and the LCRA began supplying wholesale electric power from Buchanan, and later Inks Dam, to municipalities and rural electric cooperatives.[26] GVEC and DeWitt County Electric Cooperative were among the LCRA's first rural electric customers and would remain so for the next seventy-plus years.[27] By 1940, the LCRA had completed four dams on the Lower Colorado and was providing low-cost hydropower to customers. For more than two decades, the Lower Colorado River Authority was able to keep up with growth in the area by building hydroelectric dams and keeping rates low to wholesale customers.

Transforming Members' Lives

Delivering reliable, inexpensive electric power to the members of the Guadalupe Valley Electric Cooperative was literally transformative in the impact it had on life and society. Since the nation's rural areas had been deprived of electric power when the private

Rural farm life was downright hard to keep productive back then, just like a heavy iron. Robert Caro, who wrote the biography of Lyndon B. Johnson, described this way of life as "the sad irons," featured on page 20. He used the iron to represent the story of the many struggles of Central Texas farm families in the days before rural electrification. *Courtesy of LBJ Library Online*

utilities began serving urban areas in the 1890s, residents of South Central Texas had to be introduced to the life benefits that electric power could bring. Before electricity, everything on the farm was done by hand. Those days were long gone for many families thanks to the service of GVEC.

The dream of the Guadalupe Valley Electric Cooperative began with a few farmers working together to make life better for their families and communities. Though there were many obstacles along the way, their tenacity would pay off for generations of cooperative members to come. It all started with strong people, a vision, and self-made determination. It was a work ethic and commitment to improving lives that remains evident in the philosophy of GVEC leadership today.

The establishment of the Guadalupe Valley Electric Cooperative transformed the quality of life for many rural families through teamwork, vision, and commitment to empowering the people and communities it served. Though our membership and Cooperative services are more diverse than ever before, those same values remain rooted in the work of GVEC still today.

Continuing to serve as Board president as of 2013, Lewis Borgfeld's extensive financial background and remarkably tenured experience has guided GVEC through trailblazing decisions that are firsts for the Cooperative and the electric industry.

Chapter **Two**

The Right LEADERS

Darren Schauer was a Gonzales native whose grandfather, Monroe Schauer, had been the longtime Board president of GVEC. A Texas A&M graduate who started working for the Cooperative in the summers, Schauer began his full-time career at GVEC as a marketing representative, working in such areas as satellite television, rural broadband, and demand side management. When Marcus Pridgeon was named general manager in 1993, Schauer worked as his assistant working with power supply, financing, and budgeting issues and later took on management responsibilities when he became manager of the Computer Information Services Division in 1997.[43]

When Pridgeon left for LCRA in 2003, Schauer was one of several internal candidates for the job. The Board selected Schauer, and he began his tenure as GVEC's fifth general manager and CEO in August 2003. Since that time, Schauer's progressive leadership style has led to the implementation of a strategic planning process and the formalization of an annual business and operations plan. In addition, he led the charge for defined Cooperative vision and

mission statements and established the first official set of Corporate Values that guide all employees in their service to the membership today. Schauer carried on Pridgeon's environment of openness at the Cooperative and has worked to expand it to a feeling of family among the workforce.

Schauer's passion for good service is reflected in GVEC's commitment to its fifty-six thousand member-owners and to the betterment of the communities in the thirteen Texas counties where they live. He has been instrumental in implementing a practical mentality and a culture of quality customer service at GVEC, and he has involved the Cooperative at all levels of community, state, and national organizations. Known for promoting integrity and dedication amongst GVEC's employees, he is also a firm believer in individual and team accountability. A manager for the twenty-first century, Schauer strives to encourage creativity, thinking outside the lines and trying new things. His trailblazing outlook is focused on the future and the new technologies that will make life better for GVEC member-owners today and tomorrow.

During Schauer's tenure as general manager, a significant amount of time has also been spent on developing a new power supply strategy for the future. In 2010, GVEC gave notice of termination to LCRA of its wholesale power supply contract as of 2016. Schauer has led every crucial step of the transition and stated those efforts will continue into the future. "Though my tenure here at GVEC has presented various challenges and opportunities, much of my primary focus has been on working through plans to transition from LCRA and the restructuring of our power supply strategy. This is no small task to undertake, but I am confident this move is in the best future interests of the GVEC member-owners. The move will help keep rates as stable as possible as well as build flexibility for the Cooperative to adapt more quickly to changes and mandates as the energy industry evolves."[44]

In 2003, Darren Schauer assumed the position of fifth general manager of GVEC. Credited with a progressive leadership style driven by strategic planning and operations, his passion for good service has led GVEC to provide diverse services beyond electricity and build the flexibility it needs to adapt to future challenges.

In November 2010, the GVEC Board of Directors decided not to renew the Cooperative's all-requirements contract with the Lower Colorado River Authority as of June 2016. This move would allow the Cooperative to acquire energy from diversified providers and sources. The decision was made to build the flexibility GVEC needed to quickly adapt to future energy industry challenges and mandates and keep electric rates fair for its members.
Photo courtesy of Calpine Corporation

Chapter **Three**

Aquiring ENERGY

Delivering reliable and affordable electricity has been a staple of GVEC service since the beginning and the most crucial aspect of that is acquiring energy. It all started with one robust power supplier. Over the years, changes in the wholesale power market and strategic decisions by the GVEC leadership have provided the Cooperative with expanded wholesale power purchase options to meet demand, save money, and grow more versatile for the future.

The delivery of electric power to members of GVEC is a complex coordination of generation, transmission and distribution of a product that cannot be stored once it is produced. The process is little changed since electrical pioneers such as Thomas Edison and George Westinghouse designed the Pearl Street electric system in the late nineteenth century. For GVEC, the process involves purchasing electric power on contracts from wholesale suppliers since the Cooperative does not own the generation assets such as hydroelectric dams or coal-fired steam plants that produce electricity for its members.

For much of GVEC's history, the Cooperative purchased electric power from a wholesale supplier with deep roots in the Texas public power movement. The GVEC Board and E. A. Hassman, the first general manager, negotiated a wholesale power contract in the earliest days of the Cooperative with the Lower Colorado River Authority (LCRA) to provide GVEC with electric power from a hydroelectric plant on the Guadalupe River in Gonzales County.

Throughout much of the early years of the Cooperative, GVEC was well served as an all-requirements (meaning the Cooperative purchased 100 percent of its electric power from the LCRA) customer of the Lower Colorado River Authority. The LCRA was able to deliver ample electric power from its hydroelectric generating system during the 1950s and into the 1960s. By 1962, however, the Austin-based system was supplementing its hydroelectric base load with electricity from a leased power plant in New Braunfels and a newly constructed natural gas plant in Bastrop.

In the years following World War II, GVEC was purchasing wholesale power from the LCRA almost exclusively. The relationship between GVEC and the LCRA blossomed during this postwar era, with low wholesale power rates dominating between 1945 and 1973; the growth in kilowatt-hour usage during the period meant that economies of scale produced rates that were less expensive the more members consumed.

By the 1970s, the economies of scale that GVEC and other customers were experiencing began to erode. The Arab-Israeli War in 1973 and the ensuing oil boycott by the Organization of Petroleum Exporting Countries (OPEC) ushered in a new era of energy shortages for American utilities and forced the LCRA to begin building coal-fired electric generating stations to supply base load electric power to GVEC and other Texas customers. The construction of this new generation in the late 1970s and 1980s resulted in wholesale power rate increases to GVEC and other customers. Following the authority of the Public Utilities Commission of Texas (PUC), created in 1970, every rate increase request had to be aired in a public forum. GVEC and other wholesale customers were forced to pass along its wholesale rate increases to members, who frequently voiced their opposition to the increases at contentious public hearings. The Cooperative was in essence between a rock and a hard place, serving as the bearer of bad tidings for its members concerning wholesale power price increases over which GVEC had little control.

The Lower Colorado River Authority

The booming Texas economy began to outstrip the LCRA's ability to furnish the region with inexpensive hydropower as early as the 1960s. To combat this, the LCRA began construction of its Bastrop natural gas plant in 1962. By 1970, the power supplier had tripled the size of the Bastrop plant and was building a similar natural gas unit at Marble Falls to keep up with demand.[45]

The Arab Oil Embargo in the wake of the Yom Kippur War in October 1973 created an energy crisis in North America that roiled utility markets in the United States for the next fifteen years. Domestic natural gas supplies were a casualty of the energy upheavals, and it would take federal deregulation of the industry to convince exploration companies to once again begin drilling for new supplies of gas in the 1980s.

The LCRA, like many wholesale suppliers in Texas, was hampered by natural gas shortages from 1973 on.[46] The shortages of natural gas resulted in a vicious spiral of wholesale rate increases that would continue for much of the next twenty years. Wholesale customers such as GVEC and DeWitt County Electric Cooperative were all too often cast as the middlemen in a drama that they could not control. Between 1976 and 1978, the Texas Railroad Commission ceded its utility regulatory authority to a new Public Utilities Commission of Texas (PUC), which began requiring public hearings for utilities requesting a rate increase.

With demand exceeding more than hydropower could produce, LCRA built its first major steam electric generating plant, the Sim Gideon Steam Plant in Bastrop, shown here during the final stage of construction in 1965.

Then GVEC President Monroe Schauer and General Manager Doyle Hines discuss the increased cost of purchased power and the rate changes that would impact the GVEC membership in April 1975.

In the late 1970s, the LCRA made a decision that seemed to make sense at the time. They committed to construction of the Fayette Power Project (FPP), a three-unit coal-fired generation station that would provide more than one thousand megawatts of power to the LCRA and its customers. Fueled by low-sulfur Powder River Basin coal from Wyoming, the FPP seemed to be the solution to the LCRA's capacity problems. Utilities and their financial backers believed at the time that a healthy utility had a diversified generation portfolio, consisting of coal, hydro, gas, and nuclear power sources.[47]

But the LCRA built the FPP at a time when construction financing was expensive. When Units 1 and 2 came on line in 1979 and 1980, construction interest rates and inflation were both in double digits. LCRA had to have long-term contracts with its wholesale power customers to pay for its expensive coal-fired base load generation.

A New Utility Landscape

The 1980s and 1990s were among the most difficult decades in the long history of the electric utility industry. Escalating fuel costs, which had plagued the industry since the 1970s, continued well into the 1980s. Congress and state legislatures began to advocate deregulation measures that would usher in the biggest set of changes for utilities since the Great Depression.

Fortunately, GVEC had anticipated many of the changes and had prepared the Cooperative and its members for a new utility landscape. Under the capable leadership of Lewis Borgfeld and the Board of Directors, GVEC and its management team of Doyle Hines and Marcus Pridgeon positioned the Cooperative for new opportunities at the turn of the twenty-first century.

Faster Than Anybody Else

When the LCRA's Fayette Units 1 and 2 were coming on line in 1980 and 1981 (Unit 3 went into commercial operation in 1988), the increasing cost of residential, commercial, and industrial electric power galvanized federal and state officials to revisit the longstanding regulatory compact that governed how utilities operated. Proponents of deregulation of the electric utility industry argued that competition would drive down costs for consumers.

Congress reacted to the crisis of the 1970s by passing the Public Utilities Regulatory Policy Act of 1978 (PURPA), which required electric utilities to buy power from nonregulated generators of electricity. Congress further deregulated electric utilities when it passed the National Energy Policy Act (NEPA) in 1992. NEPA allowed nonutility electric power producers access to the nation's grid of high-voltage transmission lines.

Deregulation and competition would come to the electric utility industry in fits and starts. Some states and entities, such as California, would rush into utility deregulation with disastrous results. Other experiments with deregulation and competition would move more slowly and produce lasting results. Fortunately for the state's utility industry, Texas was relatively conservative in how it proceeded on the question of deregulation and electric utility competition.

Texas deregulated its wholesale electric power market in 1995 and retail electric power markets four years later. Texas legislators, however, exempted the state's electric cooperatives and municipal electric systems

The Fayette Power Project was a joint effort of the Lower Colorado River Authority and the City of Austin. Electric energy produced at the generating plant provided more than 91 percent of the wholesale power purchased by GVEC at the time of its fifteen-year anniversary in April 1994.

from retail competition. This move put the decision to opt in to competition in the locally controlled hands of the cooperative Board of Directors and City Council members governing the municipalities. GVEC, although not a proponent of unbridled retail competition, was not afraid to compete. Marcus Pridgeon, who served as GVEC's general manager during the deregulation debate, wrote a white paper on the topic that he titled "Elephants and Zebras." The title, he said, was derived from the premise that regulated electric utilities were elephants that needed to change into zebras.

"We had to be faster than everybody else to survive," Pridgeon explained.[48]

For the LCRA, deregulation and competition was more of a threat than an opportunity. Saddled with high fixed costs for its Fayette units, the LCRA simply had to have guaranteed long-term contracts to keep operating. Pridgeon sat through some harsh and contentious meetings with the LCRA during the mid-1990s battling over wholesale power rates. The contract GVEC executed with the LCRA in 1974 was amended and extended in 1991, with an expiration date of June 24, 2016.

When the wholesale market in Texas began to change with the 1995 passage of Senate Bill 373, an active, competitive wholesale market began to develop with a number of creditworthy suppliers in the state willing to offer competitive prices and terms on bilateral power supply arrangements. This development was a step forward for the wholesale power industry, however GVEC was not able to take advantage of it due to the all-requirements contract in place with the LCRA. This would remain true until 2004 when the LCRA would begin seeking extended contracts from its customers.

Pridgeon's successor, Darren Schauer, and the GVEC Board, would have to make some of the most difficult decisions in the Cooperative's history during the next decade.

Power Supply for the Twenty-first Century

For Darren Schauer and GVEC, power supply has been the overriding issue facing the Cooperative since 2003. "This issue has involved substantial and significant decisions we have had to make in regards to the future of GVEC," he said.[49]

In 2004, the LCRA approached GVEC with a proposal to amend and extend the utility's wholesale contract. The proposal contained a provision that allowed GVEC to purchase as much as 20 percent of its annual power needs from suppliers other than the LCRA. But it also required the Cooperative to sign an extension until 2041. GVEC's Board examined the proposal and found it to be essentially the same terms the Cooperative had been operating under since the 1940s. After careful consideration, the Board rejected the proposal. It was at that time that GVEC began the process of planning to purchase its wholesale power supply in a deregulated marketplace.

In 2004 and 2005, GVEC and several other LCRA wholesale customers set about trying to convince the Authority that it needed to change its business model to reflect the new world of utility economics. GVEC and nine other wholesale power customers were concerned about the LCRA's ability to control costs,

and as a result, formed the Wholesale Power Alliance (WPA) in 2005 to negotiate with LCRA. WPA members included the cities of Boerne, Seguin, and Georgetown, the Kerrville Public Utility Board, New Braunfels Utilities, Central Texas Electric Cooperative, Fayette Electric Cooperative, and San Bernard Electric Cooperative.

"From our perspective," Schauer explains, "we wanted to hold on to that relationship with LCRA. We were willing to buy the power produced by its existing plants, but we were not going to commit to buying more power in the future if LCRA could not produce competitively."[50] The WPA represented 40 percent of the LCRA's load, and Pedernales Electric Cooperative, which was not a WPA member, constituted another 30 percent of the LCRA's load. Management upheavals at Pedernales Electric Cooperative (PEC) in 2008 and 2009 led PEC to sign the extension with the LCRA in 2009.

GVEC did not go into the new world of deregulated wholesale power lightly. With the mid-2011 deadline for informing the LCRA of its decision on a contract extension approaching, the Cooperative's Board and staff conducted an exhaustive study during 2010 with a formal Request-for-Proposal sent to a select group of financially sound and reputable industry participants. Responses ranged from private brokers to large-scale power generators and included options such as all-requirements and partial-requirements contracts, ownership in power plants, and renewable opportunities.

GVEC and its Board recognized in 2010 that the LCRA was not willing at the time to change its wholesale power pricing structure and would again require GVEC to enter into a long-term commitment. After considerable effort to negotiate and extensive studies on various power options, GVEC decided not to renew its contract as of 2016 and officially gave notice to the LCRA in November 2010. All of the other WPA members took similar action.

Darren Schauer explained that the decision to leave the Lower Colorado River Authority was difficult but necessary. He told members that significant changes had taken place in the wholesale market since 1974, and that the market had transitioned from being highly regulated by the Public Utility Commission to one that was deregulated. The LCRA did offer GVEC a contract extension that would allow the Cooperative to purchase a portion of its requirements from other sources, but Schauer noted that the extension would lock in GVEC to the LCRA contract for twenty-five years, and the majority of the Cooperative's energy requirements would come up for renewal at the same time.[51]

"Our wholesale power plan moving forward will include multiple suppliers, diversified fuel sources, and staggered terms so as not to be forced to renew our entire supply at one time, or to be locked into one supplier for a long period of time for a majority of our needs."

Board President Lewis Borgfeld noted in 2010 "the Board concluded changes in the wholesale power market offered more options than ever before to self-manage our wholesale power needs. Standing solid with a strong financial position, the timing was right to make a change. Doing so will increase the Cooperative's flexibility to adapt to potential political, economic, and technological factors affecting the electric industry more quickly than ever before, resulting in increased control over affordability."[52]

With new management in place at the LCRA's Austin headquarters in 2010, the LCRA began working to reduce their cost structure and began allowing customers who had agreed to extend their contracts to 2041 to access the competitive wholesale market, but denied customers who had not extended their contracts that same opportunity. This discriminatory treatment led GVEC to file a breach of contract claim against the LCRA. They responded with a lawsuit claiming the Cooperative was unilaterally violating its long-term contract with the intent to purchase a portion of its energy requirements from other providers beginning December 1, 2012.

GVEC General Manager and CEO Darren Schauer stated, "GVEC is highly disappointed that the LCRA has chosen to file suit instead of living up to its contractual obligations and remedying its breach. GVEC will not subject its customers to discriminatory treatment and stands ready to defend its position."[53]

After intense negotiations over a period of approximately six months, the litigation was settled in December 2012 and the agreement allowed GVEC to buy 15 percent of its power needs outside the LCRA contract in 2013, and increasing that amount of outside purchase by 5 percent a year through 2016. Schauer expressed satisfaction with the positive outcome. "I am pleased that this suit between LCRA and GVEC is no longer lingering. This agreement will allow GVEC to move forward with accessing the competitive power market for a good portion of our power requirements each year, which will result in significant savings for our membership and price certainty for the future."

The decision to change power suppliers was one of the toughest GVEC had ever had to make. But in the final analysis, GVEC had to consider what was best for the members. "When making these important decisions," Borgfeld continued, "we recognize at the end of the day GVEC members expect their lights to be on and want that service at the lowest possible cost. For those reasons, we've made confident decisions to proactively prepare the Cooperative to more readily adapt to the challenges of the future."[54]

General Manager Darren Schauer reported in January 2011: "Our wholesale power plan moving forward will include multiple suppliers, diversified fuel sources, and staggered terms so as not to be forced to renew our entire supply at one time, or to be locked into one supplier for a long period of time for a majority of our needs."[55]

By the end of 2011, the Cooperative had negotiated contracts with J. P. Morgan, American Electric Power (AEP), and NextEra Energy for the wholesale base load power it will need to purchase starting in 2016. Those initial three contracts called for a fifty-megawatt unit contingent contract with a coal-fired facility based on a fixed monthly capacity payment, and eighty megawatts of block power transactions. Contract terms are set to run from 5.5 years to 10.5 years and commence in June 2016.

Financing a Modern Cooperative

Making the bold move to self-managing its wholesale power supply would not be possible without a financially stable cooperative. Paying the millions of dollars in costs to ensure that members have access to reliable, affordable electricity is the Cooperative's major responsibility. Since its formation in 1939, the Guadalupe Valley Electric Cooperative has always enjoyed the reputation of operating as a well-run, fiscally conservative organization. That has not changed in the twenty-first century.

By their very nature, electric utilities are capital intensive. It costs money to build and maintain electric transmission and distribution systems. Since it repaid its government loans a quarter-century ago, GVEC has borrowed money in the private marketplace. As a result, the Cooperative has strived to keep its financial ratings as high as possible. That effort has paid substantial dividends since its deployment.

Thorough planning in every area of the Cooperative by the Board of Directors and management staff make it possible for GVEC to continue its history of strong financial performance. Maintaining strong financial performance and high credit ratings have allowed GVEC to make trailblazing decisions and transition itself into a twenty-first century well-rounded and diversified energy supplier for its member-owners.

In late December 2006, Standard & Poor's (S&P), the world's foremost source of credit ratings, investment research, risk, and evaluation of data, awarded GVEC an A+ stable rating. S&P cited GVEC's good debt service coverage, adequate liquid assets to meet infrastructure needs, and a strong equity position to finance future capital projects.

The A+ S&P rating confirmed GVEC's outstanding financial position, which put it among the highest-rated distribution cooperatives in the nation. More importantly, the rating allowed GVEC to borrow money for capital projects at better interest rates than other utilities. "The benefits of GVEC receiving this rating have already started to surface," said General Manager Darren Schauer. "These benefits translate into substantial savings, year after year, for our member-owners."[56]

The Cooperative followed up its S&P rating with further achievements. In April 2010, GVEC earned an F1+ short term and A+ long-term rating from Fitch Ratings, another of the world's top credit rating agencies. Fitch Ratings cited GVEC's "strong financial performance, manageable leverage, and solid equity levels."[57]

The high short-term and long-term ratings allowed GVEC to take advantage of a Commercial Paper Program (CPP), a method of short-term, unsecured borrowing that would help save the Cooperative significant money in interest costs over time.

Darren Schauer reported in 2012 that GVEC's participation in the CPP had allowed the Cooperative to recognize more than $1.8 million in short-term interest savings, compared to other short-term financing available from traditional cooperative sources. "Savings like this contribute to keeping electric rates as low as possible," Darren Schauer explained.[58]

From a long-term perspective, Schauer told member-owners that the Cooperative had taken $40 million in GVEC bonds to market in December 2011. At the 3.77 percent interest rate available because of the Cooperative's A+ S&P rating, GVEC would recognize more than $3.3 million in savings compared to the next lowest rate.

"GVEC continues to take a progressive, yet vigilant, approach to debt management in order to save you money," Schauer told members.[59] Today, GVEC is maintaining its strong financial performance, and only plans to get better, as this will be key to future savings opportunities for the member-owners as the wholesale power market continues to change.

GVEC has transitioned itself over the past seventy-five years from a traditional cooperative to a twenty-first century energy supplier owned by its members. As the Board of Directors and General Manager Darren Schauer continue to make trailblazing decisions in regards to the Cooperative self-managing its power supply strategy as of 2016, reliability and affordability for members remains the top priority along with developing the flexibility to quickly adapt to evolving energy industry challenges and regulations. One of the most significant of those challenges is the dependable delivery of services for a continuously growing service area.

By the late 2000s, Cooperative operations had grown to depend largely on the efficient and effective use of technology. GVEC has made it a staple of service to upgrade equipment as well as implement new software and processes when and where it makes sense and makes a significant difference in the level of service to members.

Chapter **Four**

Delivery of SERVICES

For GVEC, delivery of valuable services is its core reason for existence. Growing more diverse every year, not only has the Cooperative experienced change regarding the physical delivery of power, it has also cultivated continuous growth of its service territory and evolved with it. With each new challenge, GVEC continues to redefine the value of Cooperative service to its members and communities.

At the end of the day, reliable delivery of electric power to rural members living in South Central Texas has been the overriding historical work of the Guadalupe Valley Electric Cooperative. Getting the job done has meant constant focus on strengthening the electric system and its support services, spurring growth in members and demand, and evolving operations over time as the Cooperative landscape changes.

Strengthening the Electric System and Supporting Services

Securing a power source and building primary distribution lines to serve the Cooperative's first members occupied GVEC through much of its first decade of existence. The end of World War II in 1945 found the Cooperative scrambling to meet the demand from existing customers and the thousands of Guadalupe Valley residents who wanted electric power for their homes, farms, and businesses.

1950s and 1960s

The Cooperative borrowed more than $1 million from REA to energize seven hundred miles of line to serve more than sixteen hundred members in the years immediately following the war and experienced rapid growth during the 1950s. By this time, GVEC crews were building sophisticated new substations to handle power purchased from the Cooperative's wholesale supplier. This included one in McQueeney and one seven miles north of Gonzales at Ottine, both energized in 1954.[60]

The Cooperative itself was naturally growing as its distribution lines reached more and more consumers. In June 1956, GVEC unveiled architects' drawings of the new Seguin Area Office, located just west of the city limits on U.S. 90.[61] That summer, REA approved a $1.145-million loan application that would allow GVEC to build 132 miles of distribution line to serve an additional eight hundred consumers beginning in 1957. The loan application also provided for additional improvements to the system, including new substations.

"The use of electricity on our system seems to increase at a constant rate," Edgar H. Zuehl, Cooperative Board member from 1948 to 1977, explained to members. "When our lines were first

Opened in 1956 and located at 1400 West Kingsbury Street, the GVEC Seguin Area Office served members until a new facility was constructed adjacent to the original location in 2009.

Edgar Zuehl, GVEC Board Member from 1948-1977, reports on the increase in demand of electricity on the GVEC system in the 1950s.

Energy demand and bricks-and-mortar growth of the system during the 1970s and 1980s included construction of numerous substations to serve the Cooperative's growing service area. This created an environment that allowed industry, including one of the first electric-arc steel mills in Texas, Structural Metals, Inc., which would later become Commercial Metals Company or CMC Steel Texas, to thrive in the region.

Energy demand and bricks-and-mortar growth also led to the necessity of a more formal planning process. A 1973 long-range system study laid the groundwork for the construction of a 138,000-volt transmission line from the Seguin Substation to the Structural Metals' (CMC's) electric arc minimill in Seguin. GVEC had built a 69,000-volt line to serve the growing Seguin area ten years before; growth of the steel mill—the only such facility in Texas on a cooperative system—necessitated the upgrading in 1975 that was overseen by then Electric System Manager Lewis Eckols.[63] The Cooperative's kilowatt-hour growth during the 1970s and early 1980s mirrored that of an investor-owned utility rather than that of a rural electric cooperative. GVEC was stable enough financially to build its own transmission lines, at a time when most rural electric cooperatives in the nation relied on Generation and Transmission (G&T) Cooperatives to build power plants and transmission lines. Investing in its own transmission lines gave the Cooperative more control over ensuring the quality delivery of electrons into its service area; an important aspect to member service.

The 1980s saw the continued implementation of a twenty-year work plan covering the period from 1972 to 1992 guiding GVEC management in making decisions. The rapid rate of population increases necessitated new line and substation construction as well as additional buildings, equipment, and personnel throughout the decade.

The existing Gonzales headquarters building was used to maximize efficiency for office space while a new building was constructed immediately north

built, the engineers designed them on the basis of an estimate of fifty kilowatt-hours use per member per month. Many people thought at the time that this estimate was entirely too high, and would never be reached."[62]

In fact, Zuehl noted, the kilowatt-hour usage had long exceeded fifty kWh per member per month and was approaching three hundred kWh per member per month in 1956.

GVEC grew to almost ten thousand members served by three thousand miles of line by 1963. The more than 200 percent increase in the use of electric energy by members, fueled by the purchase of such appliances as electric refrigerators, stoves, and washing machines, as well as electric motors for the performance of chores around the ranch or farm, was synonymous with progress in the 1950s and 1960s.

GVEC borrowed $2 million from REA to build a sixty-nine-thousand-volt transmission line to serve the growing Seguin area in 1963. By the mid-1960s, the Cooperative employed as many as seventy line crew workers who built more than nine hundred miles of line during the era.

GVEC was among very few distribution cooperatives financially stable enough to construct its own transmission lines in the 1960s. Extra-long poles were required for the new 69,000 volt transmission line, which were a first for the GVEC line crews.

A work in progress, the new transmission line marched across the rural Seguin area to help serve growth in members and demand. Today, GVEC continues to build and maintain its own transmission and distribution lines.

of the office to house the Line Material and Resale Departments as well as the Technical Service Department.[64] Plans were also made to tie the GVEC offices in Seguin and Schertz to the computer at the Gonzales office during 1980 making it possible for data processing to be entered from all areas and be immediately visible in Gonzales. During this time, the Cooperative expected to add additional substations at one per year for the next twelve to fifteen years and expansion of the Schertz Substation and construction of the Cibolo Substation would be completed. Attention was also given to the Marion Substation and Lake Wood Substation, the point of delivery for receiving power from the Guadalupe Blanco River Authority's six hydroelectric damns along the Guadalupe River: the result of a new twenty-year power agreement contract signed in January 1980.

In the period from 1990 to 1999, the Cooperative's growth in new accounts, energy sales, and plant additions skyrocketed. Over just ten years, the Cooperative added 9,855 new accounts, equating to a growth rate of 33.5 percent. During this same period, GVEC's annual energy sales increased by 351,338,941 kilowatt-hours, or 43.4 percent. On January 1, 1990, the Co-op total plant was valued at $72,453,121 and it closed the century at $134,001,972.00. Much of this growth could be attributed to the Cooperative's strong industrial and commercial account base at the time.

By the time the 2000s came around, it was made clear by then General Manager Marcus Pridgeon that every employee was important to the level of service GVEC was providing.

In 2002, Pridgeon implemented a report card system designed to make each employee aware of how well GVEC was keeping the lights on. Each morning, a report was generated that logged every outage and every blink across the entire system for the prior twenty-four-hour period. Pridgeon proclaimed about the practice, "It keeps us better informed, it makes us work as a team, and it also makes us all aware of how important each individual is in accomplishing our goal of keeping the lights on."[65]

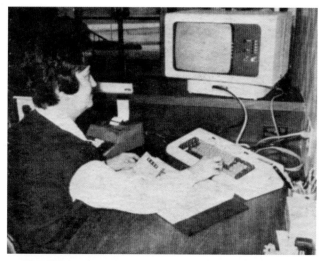

In 1980, networking the computer systems between Gonzales, Seguin, and Schertz allowed for data processing duties to be shared by all offices. This made the work of Cashier Maple Remschel, and many other employees, much more efficient and productive.

Left to right, then GVEC General Manager Doyle Hines, GBRA General Manager John Specht, and GBRA Operations Manager Greg Roth discuss arrangements for the delivery of hydroelectric power from GBRA via the twenty-year power agreement signed in 1980.

By 2008, GVEC was well underway adding multiple communications towers, deploying mobile wireless communication for improved response times, and adding a new fiber communication system to enhance field communications and monitoring capabilities.

From 2008 through 2012, the Cooperative had grown from 472 miles of underground distribution line to a total of 513. Overhead distribution line had grown from 7,757 miles to 8,068 miles and GVEC was serving 71,164 meters.[66] Line maintenance activities consisted of clearing hundreds of miles of rights-of-ways on multiple circuits per year, inspecting thousands of distribution and transmission poles annually, and upgrading equipment and technology when and where it was necessary for continuous strengthening of the GVEC electric system.

Milestones of Cooperative Growth

During the first fifteen years of GVEC's existence, growth of the cooperative primarily came from the recruitment of new members to living an easier life through electricity. The growth of the Texas farm economy was also partially responsible for corresponding growth of revenues and kWh sales at GVEC.

From the 1950s to today, five significant milestones have greatly contributed to growth in members and demand for the Cooperative. The first was internal

Since the early years, the GVEC Resale Shop provided electrical supplies, wiring materials, and recommendations for safe projects to the public. Located both in Seguin (at the Area office) and in Gonzales, a new location was opened in 1995 off Oakland Avenue, just behind the Gonzales office off Sarah DeWitt Drive. Today, this area houses GVEC.net operations.

By 2008, GVEC was adding multiple communications towers and deploying mobile wireless and fiber technology. These measures continue working today to enhance internal communications and remote monitoring capabilities as well as improve response times.

and involved the Cooperative's embrace of electric heating and cooling. The remaining factors are all external and include continuous expansion in the Western service area, consolidation with a neighboring co-op, responding to the significant discovery of the Eagle Ford Shale oil and gas play (area of exploration), and serving one of the largest industrial loads in the region.

Milestones of Growth:
Embracing Electric Heating and Cooling

From the very beginning, GVEC has had forward-thinking leaders from the Board of Directors to the general manager. With the mindset of delivering reliable, affordable power at the forefront, it was known that the way to reduce overall cost of electricity was to get more people to use it at regular intervals. Doing so would create a more stable year-round demand for electricity and therefore make it more economical to purchase power. In 1955, GVEC adopted an All-Electric Home Rate to encourage members to use electric power for heating, cooking, and water heating. The rate was attractive enough that thirty-one homes on the Cooperative's system qualified by implementing all-electric features such as electric ranges, air conditioning, and heating in their homes by September 1956.[67]

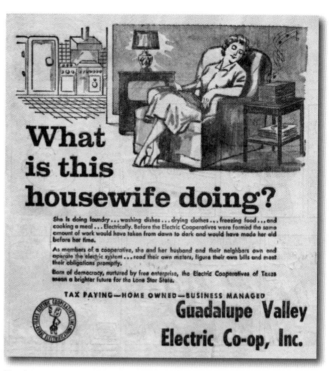

To raise awareness and create interest in electricity and the Co-op, billboards and print ads like this one were used to clearly communicate the conveniences of living an energized lifestyle and the benefits of GVEC membership.

One homeowner told the Cooperative that his family had heated their home with firewood, kerosene, butane, and finally electricity. Members in the late 1950s and early 1960s also were rapidly adding window air conditioners to cool their homes during the summer. In the spring of 1958, GVEC began urging its members to use space heaters to heat their homes in winter and air conditioners to cool them in summer.[68]

When Doyle Hines was hired as GVEC's new power use advisor in November 1958, his primary job was to encourage members to convert to electric heating and cooling. As power use advisor and then general manager for more than a quarter-century, Hines was instrumental in establishing GVEC as one of the first Texas cooperatives to achieve the distinction of being both a summer and a winter peaker.

In the 1950s, the embrace of heating and cooling was a major milestone in the early growth of the Cooperative. Efforts to encourage the use of electricity through building and maintaining a modern electric home would result in a more stable year-round demand for electricity and therefore make it more economical to purchase power for the membership.

The Schertz area office was opened at 900 Curtiss Avenue on July 28, 1968, to serve the growing western portion of the GVEC service area. The office was equipped with a drive-thru and modern electric kitchen showpiece.

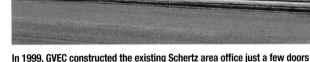

In 1999, GVEC constructed the existing Schertz area office just a few doors down at 908 Curtiss Avenue.

Milestones of Growth:
Expansion in the Western Area

GVEC generally refers to its service territory as split into two regions. The first is the Western Territory: more suburban in nature and includes Guadalupe, Wilson, and parts of Comal Counties. Second is the Eastern Territory, which is the more rural portion and primarily includes members within Gonzales, DeWitt, and Lavaca Counties.

The Western Territory has historically been the largest in terms of general population and density of members for GVEC. The furthest boundary is located on the outskirts of San Antonio, Texas, and includes the City of Schertz: the area chosen in 1931 for the establishment of Randolph Air Force Base. Opened to train pilots for the fledgling U.S. Army Air Corps, Randolph—named for an Austin pilot killed in an early air crash—trained pilots and instructors during World War II. During the postwar era, it continued to train pilots, and in 1958, the Air Force relocated the Air Training Command (ATC) headquarters from Scott Air Force Base to the big base located just northeast of San Antonio.

The decision to relocate was important to GVEC as it opened the door to military families moving into the area, which helped create density in the early years and further electric demand. This satisfied two of the leading aims of Cooperative management at the time.

Spurred from proactively planning for growth in the western region of the service area, the La Vernia office was opened in October 2005 at 13849 U.S. Highway 87 West, complete with a GVEC Home appliance showroom.

Joined by Board Directors, staff, and folks from the La Vernia community, General Manager Darren Schauer started a GVEC tradition of cutting the wire, instead of ribbon, for new facilities at the La Vernia office grand opening.

Former Seguin Mayor Betty Ann Matthies and members of the Seguin Area Chamber of Commerce were among the crowd joining Chamber President Shawn Martinez, GVEC Board President Lewis Borgfeld, and General Manager Darren Schauer among other directors and employees at the Seguin office grand opening in 2009.

More members needing and using more electricity would work to the benefit of all GVEC consumers to lower wholesale power purchase costs per member.

Growth within the Western Territory has remained consistent over the years. Cities such as La Vernia, Cibolo, and Schertz became known as bedroom communities due to their access to the San Antonio metropolitan area. Increasing need for services resulted in the decision to locate a new office in Schertz, which opened on July 28, 1968, at 900 Curtiss Avenue and cultivated a remodel of the Seguin area office at 1400 West Kingsbury Street that would eventually expand once again adding a materials

department and warehouse space by 1982. In 1999, GVEC constructed a new Schertz area office and warehouse just down the road at 908 Curtiss Avenue, which continues to serve members today.

By 2005, under the strategic leadership of General Manager Darren Schauer and the Board of Directors, GVEC had begun proactively planning for growth in the region over the next twenty years. With customer-focused service as an integral part of the business plan, the Cooperative opened a new customer service office in October 2005 at 13849 U.S. Highway 87 West in La Vernia, complete with a GVEC Home Services Showroom.[69]

Over 65 percent of the membership resided in the Guadalupe County area by the 2008 time frame. Internal studies estimated growth in members and meters potentially doubling by 2025, which spurred the demand for additional service space and more efficient operations. As a result of these studies, a new Seguin customer service office was opened at 927 North Highway 46 in April 2009. Plans were also drawn for a new Western Operations Center to be located on a thirty-two-acre tract of land at the intersection of Nickerson Farms Road and the IH-10 West frontage road in Seguin; the geographic center of the western service area.

The Seguin office located at 927 North Highway 46 was opened in April 2009 complete with the largest GVEC Home Services Showroom to date.

A groundbreaking was held in the spring of 2010 and the state-of-the-art Western Operations Center was opened in May 2011. It would serve as the hub of operations for the western portion of GVEC's service area and play a significant role in reducing area outage response times and increasing operational efficiencies. Read more about the features and benefits of the Western Operations Center in Chapter 5.

Milestones of Growth:
Exploring Consolidation with a
Neighboring Cooperative

By the time GVEC celebrated its fiftieth anniversary in 1988, the Cooperative was well on its way to reaching the size and shape as it exists today. The strategy of building and upgrading electric distribution and transmission lines to serve the Cooperative's members was as valid in the 1980s and 1990s as it was in the 1930s and 1940s. But by the late 1980s, service area growth was at a plateau. Demographics dictated that many small farms were going out of business and being consolidated into larger, more efficient operations. Members, thanks to the Cooperative's focus on energy efficiency, became much more efficient consumers themselves.

Acquisition of other consumers was pursued throughout the 1990s and reached fruition in 2002 by a merger with DeWitt County Electric Cooperative, more informally known as DeWitt Electric Cooperative (DEC).

All electric utilities operate best when they can maximize economies of scale to consumers' benefit. DEC had been organized in 1938 at the same time as GVEC, and by the 1990s was serving a much smaller consumer base than GVEC, which would make it challenging in the times ahead to keep rates as economical as possible for its members.

The driving force behind consolidation was the 1995 deregulation of the wholesale market for electricity in Texas. Both the federal government and state governments had reacted to the energy shortages of the 1970s by passing legislation to deregulate the wholesale electricity marketplace; the resulting disruptions in supply and pricing from competition caused difficulties for utilities that had long been regulated. Marcus Pridgeon recalled that the early years of competition were not at all friendly to residential ratepayers in Texas or elsewhere. Pridgeon and the GVEC Board understood that the most cost efficient way to deliver electricity to consumers would involve making GVEC as efficient as possible in the way it did business. Consolidation was one method to achieve those efficiencies.[70]

The DeWitt County Electric Cooperative, more informally known as the DeWitt Electric Cooperative, was established at the same time as GVEC and served a close, but much smaller member base. This made the cooperative a prime candidate for a merger with GVEC which would result in savings for all area cooperative members.

DeWitt County Electric Cooperative was led by General Manager Jim Springs. He began discussions in 1992 with then GVEC General Manager Doyle Hines regarding a proposed consolidation which was initially declined by the DeWitt membership. Springs remained at the helm of the Cooperative through the second attempt at consolidation, which began in 1998.

Stronger Than Ever To Serve You

gvec
Guadalupe Valley Electric Cooperative
2001 Annual Report

In a message entitled "Stronger Together," then GVEC General Manager Marcus Pridgeon and Board President Lewis Borgfeld commented on the consolidation in the first Annual Report to the new membership saying, "We are a stronger electric cooperative today. It wasn't an easy task, and it wasn't a quick process, but the benefits of this consolidation far outweigh any obstacles that we encountered." Representing the newer, stronger GVEC on the 2001 Annual Report cover from left to right was new GVEC Administrative Division Manager Jim Springs and GVEC General Manager Marcus Pridgeon.

On January 1, 2002, GVEC and the DeWitt Electric Cooperative consolidated forming a new Guadalupe Valley Electric Cooperative with an eleven-member Board of Directors. Seated, left to right: David R. Dennis—Cibolo District 8; Robert J. Werner, Shiner—District 1; W. A. (Bill) Lott, Nixon—District 5; James Hastings, Stockdale—District 6; Vice-President Melvin E. Strey, La Vernia—District 7; President Lewis Borgfeld, Cibolo—District 2; Secretary-Treasurer Robert A. Young, Jr., Gonzales—District 4; Don Williams, Yoakum—District 10; David Warzecha, Cuero—District 11; Henry Schmidt, Jr., Gonzales—District 3; and Dr. Tom DeKunder, Schertz—District 9. Standing, left to right: Advisory Directors Tilford Steinmann, Yoakum; Al Janak, Yoakum; Tim Voelkel, Nordheim; Tracy Metting, Yorktown; and Robert Moore, Meyersville.

GVEC and DeWitt Electric Cooperative had long been good neighbors, and Doyle Hines and Jim Springs, the longtime general manager of DeWitt Electric Cooperative, had been good friends for years. Springs was never a believer that there needed to be an electric cooperative located every thirty miles in rural Texas, and he and Hines often discussed the possibility of consolidation during the 1980s. In 1992, GVEC's Board approached DEC's Board about a merger. The numbers showed that there would be a great deal of savings for DEC members in the short term and that the economies of scale would benefit all of the Cooperative members in the long term.[71]

But the loss of autonomy clearly concerned some members of the DEC Board, who campaigned against the merger. When the matter came to a vote by the DEC membership at the 1992 annual meeting, it was defeated. But the measure had opened eyes in DeWitt County. GVEC rates were lower than those of DEC, and GVEC had industrial accounts that helped balance the residential rates.[72]

The DeWitt Electric Cooperative restructured its Board in 1994, reducing the number of Board members from twelve to seven. The DEC briefly studied a merger with Karnes Electric Cooperative and Victoria Electric Cooperative, both neighboring electric cooperatives, but nothing ever came of the initiative. Negotiations between DEC and GVEC would be put on the back burner until the late 1990s.

Milestones of Growth:
Consolidation Comes to Fruition

In 1998, Marcus Pridgeon, then GVEC general manager, and Jim Springs, DeWitt Electric Cooperative (DEC) general manager, began discussing revisiting the 1992 failed consolidation discussions. This time, they took it to both memberships and commissioned the drafting of a new set of articles of consolidation. Studies continued to show the benefits of consolidation for both Cooperatives. A new, eleven-member Board of Directors would replace the nine-member GVEC Board and seven-member DEC Board. Two of the members on the new Board would come from the old DEC Board; the other five members of the DeWitt Electric Cooperative Board would serve as advisory members to the new Board until their term expired.[73]

The GVEC membership approved consolidation at the Cooperative's 2000 annual meeting in June; DEC members followed suit at their annual meeting in August at the VFW Hall in Cuero. DeWitt Electric Cooperative members approved the consolidation with a 90 percent supermajority vote.[74] The consolidation took place on January 1, 2002. With this merger, a new Guadalupe Valley Electric Cooperative was formed with the addition of 8,511 billed consumers, 95,936,855 kilowatt per hour sales and a total revenue of $8,741,843 in its first year, 13 miles of transmission line, 2,107 miles of overhead and 4 miles of underground distribution line, thirty new employees, and it's Cuero customer service facility at 909 East Broadway.

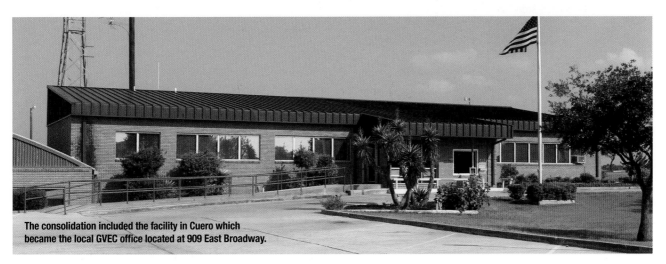

The consolidation included the facility in Cuero which became the local GVEC office located at 909 East Broadway.

The consolidation ensured the most efficient delivery of electric power to the members of both Cooperatives, and was a manifestation of the best of the cooperative spirit. As members had cooperated back in 1938 to form both GVEC and DeWitt Electric Cooperatives, they cooperated at the dawn of the twenty-first century to come together to make sure residents of rural South Central Texas would enjoy low-cost electric power for generations to come. This would be especially important as the region ushered into a population boom driven by one of the largest natural gas and oil field discoveries of the century.

Milestones of Growth: Discovery of the Eagle Ford Shale

The two-lane gravel road that runs past the late GVEC member Robert Meischen's farm in rural DeWitt County could serve as a poster for the mesquite country of South Central Texas. Meischen Road sits in a triangle bounded by Yorktown, Kenedy, and Stockdale, and by the look of it, the farmhouse Meischen and his wife built seventy-five years ago hasn't changed all that much in three-quarters of a century.

The Eagle Ford Shale gas and oil play (area of exploration) is centrally located in the GVEC territory. Gonzales and DeWitt Counties were among the top five oil producing counties in Texas in 2013 according to the Texas Railroad Commission.

Enterprise Partners' natural gas processing plant in Yoakum came online in 2012. It is just one example of the large oil-and-gas-related electric loads GVEC has supported since the discovery of the Eagle Ford Shale in 2008.

But look closely to the south, and you'll see a massive oil rig rising out of the South Texas scrub. Listen carefully, and you'll hear the rumble of an oil rig or a tanker truck long before it roars down Meischen Road.

DeWitt and Gonzales Counties are included in the ground zero area for one of the biggest oil plays in Texas in more than a generation. The Eagle Ford Shale curls across South and Central Texas like a backward "L," and the resulting boom is transforming the economy of much of South Central Texas.

The Lone Star State has been one of the nation's major oil and gas producers ever since the Spindletop Gusher blew back in 1901, but the oil boom ushered in by shale oil and gas is perhaps the biggest in the state since the 1950s. Shale deposits are being tapped by new drilling technologies involving fracturing the deposits with sand and water and drilling horizontally across the deposit.

Oil and gas production from the Eagle Ford Shale, much of it in DeWitt, Gonzales, and Karnes Counties, has increased exponentially since 2005, and one producer, Enterprise Products Partners L.P., moves some 380,000 barrels of product a day through its Eagle Ford pipeline system. Enterprise has already become GVEC's second-largest industrial customer.[75]

The Shale discovery brought with it large oil and gas companies establishing new area operations. GVEC responded to the need for additional infrastructure by working with these prominent and successful long-term businesses to negotiate mutually beneficial deals encouraging growth as well as protecting

The DeWitt Industrial Park located on Highway 183 just outside Cuero, owned by GVEC, met the needs of many new businesses supplying support services for the large Eagle Ford Shale oil and gas companies.

the best interests of member-owners. Much of the necessary infrastructure was underwritten by oil and gas members which added to the benefit of providing members with greater access to power in more rural areas where it would not typically be economically feasible to establish service.

In addition to greater access to power, the booming activity proved beneficial for the communities served by GVEC as well. Towns such as Cuero were bursting at the seams with needs to accommodate economic boosting activities such as lodging needs for families and jobs for family members of Eagle Ford workers. Support services for Eagle Ford oil and gas companies also had the need to establish operations close to the main facilities, which resulted in healthy prospects for real estate markets and community developments.

From 2011 to 2013, GVEC built five hundred miles of three-phase electric line and eight new substations to serve the addition of approximately one thousand new commercial meters as well as hundreds of new residential meters. The discovery of the Eagle Ford Shale has proven to be both challenging and rewarding for GVEC and its member-owners.

Many in Texas think the Eagle Ford Shale is just a preview of the energy future for Texas and the United States in the twenty-first century. And while the oil and gas boom brings huge economic benefits to the Cooperative and the communities it serves, it also requires GVEC to pay the closest attention to its operations and maintenance programs to ensure that the oil and gas producers have all the electric power they need to bring the riches of the Eagle Ford to market.

From 2011 to 2013, GVEC built five hundred miles of three-phase electric line and eight substations to serve the addition of approximately one thousand new commercial meters and hundreds of new residential meters stemming from the Eagle Ford Shale activity.

Serving the Largest Industrial Load in the Region

The Eagle Ford Shale growth has brought with it nearly a thousand new meters for GVEC. Major oil and gas companies such as Enterprise Crude Pipeline and Kinder Morgan joined other large commercial and industrial members including CMC Metals and Motorola (now known as Continental) that have established operations within the Guadalupe Valley: strengthening their local communities as well as the Cooperative. In fact, more than half of GVEC's energy sales are made to commercial and industrial customers in the agribusiness, production goods, healthcare, and public facilities segments of the economy. Some prominent accounts over the years include Tyson Foods in Seguin, Evenin' Star Boot Company in Gonzales, Gonzales Warm Springs Rehabilitation Hospital in Ottine, Calmaine Foods, Inc., in Waelder, and Kitchen Pride Mushroom Farms in Gonzales, with most of these companies still customers today. Some of the major players added to the mix in the last twenty-five years have been Caterpillar in Seguin, Gonzales Healthcare Systems, Schertz/Cibolo/Universal City ISD, Central Texas Ingredients (aka Adams Extract), and EOG Resources, which became one of the Cooperative's largest industrial loads in 2013. This was a testament to both the load and population growth spurred by the oil and gas activity surrounding the discovery of the Eagle Ford Shale.

Kitchen Pride Mushroom Farms operates a state-of-the-art growing and distribution facility out of Gonzales and has been a member of GVEC for over twenty years.

A Moment In Time:
The Personal Side of Commercial Accounts

At the dawn of 2013, only a handful of employees could claim they had worked with the Cooperative as long as thirty to forty years. Even fewer of those folks have worked as many positions and experienced changes in the GVEC membership as Gerald Moltz, commercial accounts manager. Starting as a groundman trainee in December 1971 and working various positions over the years such as lineman and member services advisor among others, Moltz has played a primary role in establishing many of the large commercial and industrial accounts GVEC serves today. He says the greatest hurdle in the job over the years is getting the job done in the time frame desired by the new customer. "The biggest challenge revolves around getting service to accommodate their needs. Most customers want their service quickly because it is part of the basics to start operations, but there are many variables in the process including things like obtaining easements that can sometimes cause a delay in moving forward as quickly as you would like."

Serving GVEC and its members for over forty years, Gerald Moltz is known by his many residential and commercial customers for his passion to help others and his extensive knowledge of electricity and energy efficiency. He takes pride in knowing he is making a difference in peoples' lives.

Even so, Moltz says the process of getting service to a new customer leads to the biggest reward of the job. "There's nothing like energizing lines for a customer knowing that you and your team made a difference for not just this new company, but also the people and communities it will serve."[76]

It was this dedication to his customers and passion for good service that earned him the coveted General Manager's Award from Darren Schauer in 2011 and the honor by Texas Electric Cooperatives for working forty years with no lost-time injury.

Moltz says that no matter what position he has held, the job has always been about relationships with the people. "There have been times when I hadn't seen someone in three or four years. Even if I was in a different position, they would

In 2011, Gerald Moltz earned the coveted General Manager's Award from Darren Schauer for his many years of dedication and outstanding levels of service to the members of GVEC. In the same year, he was also recognized by TEC, GVEC's statewide affiliate, for forty years on the job with no lost-time injury.

call me back to ask questions and rely on my help. They knew me, they trusted me, and wanted my input on whatever it was they were working on at the time. To work here, you have to have that sincere desire to help people and it means a lot to know that came through."[77]

There may be no better words than a "sincere desire to help people" to describe the enduring cooperative tradition of good people working together to make a difference in the lives of their neighbors and communities.

Calmaine Foods, Inc., served by GVEC since the early 2000s, is the largest producer and marketer of shell eggs in the United States and operates expansive facilities out of Waelder and Flatonia.

The Evolution of Lines and Line Work

As all aspects of the Cooperative continue to grow, the importance of evolution in equipment, safety, and training for GVEC line work becomes ever more paramount. Though it is not the only necessary element of providing good service, line work is one of the most crucial components of building and maintaining a strong electric system.

Line Work Evolution:
Changes in the Tools of the Trade

When GVEC linemen built their first overhead lines in the 1940s, it was backbreaking work. The image of linemen-farmers using pike poles to push distribution poles into place and wooden spools to string line overhead are part of the story of rural electrification.

According to now retired GVEC linemen, things began to change in the 1970s. Ronnie Foreman, who retired from GVEC in 2008, started working for the Cooperative in 1965. He trained under legendary local linemen such as Carl Alsup and Lloyd Perkins, Thomas Coor and Caroll Albright, men who wore cowboy hats on the job and used pike poles and A-frame trucks to set distribution line. Foreman remembers learning how to climb poles and the hard work involved in hand tamping and shoveling off pole sets.[78]

Foreman and other linemen recalled that the Cooperative completely upgraded its fleet between 1972 and 1987. Hydraulic bucket trucks revolutionized the way line crews at GVEC worked, allowing the construction and maintenance of distribution lines to be far more efficient and safer than in the past.

When 2013 GVEC Engineering and Operations Division Manager and Chief Operating Officer Bobby Christmas started with the Cooperative in October 1981 as an apprentice lineman, GVEC had two bucket trucks, one assigned to right-of-way work and the second assigned to a maintenance line crew. Christmas was assigned a new material-handling bucket truck in 1990, and he realized it was a far safer piece of equipment than the older generation of manual material-handling trucks in use.

Every step of line work in the early years was manual as these GVEC linemen in 1953 demonstrate.

The use of hydraulic technology would forever change the productivity of line work as shown with this crew building a new substation in 1964.

From left, former Meter and Radio Superintendent Billy Mikesh; Seguin Line Superintendent Ronnie Foreman, Gonzales Line Superintendent Tommy Schurig, and Apparatus Superintendent Larry Fortune were among a team of supervisors who experienced revolutionary technological changes in GVEC operations during their time.

Over the years, Christmas and GVEC line crews have seen major changes in truck capabilities, ergonomics, and the way trucks were set up. Of course, all of those changes increased the price of bucket trucks from $100,000 in the 1980s to $250,000 and up today.

"Those trucks made it easier for linemen to do their jobs," Christmas said in a 2013 interview.[79]

But even with hydraulic bucket trucks, much of the fleet wasn't air-conditioned until 1995 and later. Trucks back in the 1980s and 1990s still had AM radios and old-time linemen swore that they could get a fix on line faults by listening for static on the radios. Crews from the 1980s and 1990s also transitioned to the use of two-way radios, and then laptop computers and cell phones that kept them in contact with the Cooperative's Control Center in Gonzales.[80]

Hydraulic line equipment has evolved over the last fifty years making construction and maintenance far more efficient and safer for each generation of GVEC crews.

Underground Coordinator and former Schertz Area Line Superintendent Gary Wilson has seen major changes since he went to work for GVEC in 1984. In his early years, line crews knew where every pay phone in the territory was located. His first cell phone was a bag phone, and by the 1990s, he typically communicated with dispatchers by fax machine. When the Cooperative upgraded its 1980s model System Control and Data Acquisition (SCADA) system with digital technology early in the twenty-first century, some of the line crews were hesitant to rely on the new technology. But overall, he said, "GVEC has always been on the progressive end of change."[81]

Underground Coordinator and former Schertz Area Line Superintendent Gary Wilson experienced the Cooperative's first use of cell phone technology in the 1980s as well as the transition into using automated line monitoring systems; all a part of a progressive mindset inherent to GVEC.

Line Work Evolution:
Safety Becomes Paramount

The advent of bucket trucks and the transition from twelve kV to twenty-five kV voltages dictated that safety became a principal focus with GVEC and its line crews. Hands-on rubber gloving thirty feet in the air meant that the slightest thing going wrong could turn into a life-threatening situation in seconds. During his thirty-plus years with the Cooperative, Bobby Christmas has worked closely with the apprenticeship program, to ensure that linemen are fully trained and accredited.[82]

GVEC takes a much more formal approach to linemen apprenticeship training in the twenty-first century than it did in earlier years. Christmas noted that attention to detail in safety training is there for a reason. "At any given moment," he said, "a life can end. We make a mistake, and it could cost a life or a serious injury. Every minute of every day, we want to know that our guys are working safe."[83]

Line Work Evolution:
New Construction and
Maintenance Techniques

Safety has been joined with new construction and maintenance techniques over the years. With the growing membership in the western end of the GVEC service area, the Cooperative has become a leader in installing underground distribution lines. New residential subdivisions in areas like Schertz, Cibolo, New Braunfels, and La Vernia demand a certain amount of aesthetics in landscaping and design, and residents don't particularly want their view marred by electric power poles.

By 2000, GVEC's Underground Crew was installing and maintaining more than 200 miles of underground distribution across the western part of the service area. GVEC had made its first forays into underground distribution in the Schertz area in the late 1960s, and has increased its underground distribution to 745 miles of line today. As the Cooperative approached its seventy-fifth anniversary, it was in the process of

By 2013, GVEC crews were maintaining almost 750 miles of underground distribution lines and beginning upgrades to modernize and automate the original lines that were a first for the Cooperative in the 1960s.

With ever-increasing voltages, one of the most important elements of safety in line work has been the evolution of personal protective equipment. Line workers such as Seguin Line Superintendent Keith Boenig, approach every project with the belief that "I am my brother's keeper"; a constant reminder that proper equipment and teamwork can and does save lives.

Regardless of serving in the past or present or the equipment and processes they've used, the one thing that has not changed from the beginning of line work is the pride all GVEC linemen have in doing "whatever it takes" to keep the lights on.

doing a cable change out for much of its early system to modernize and automate underground switching that must still be performed. Today's new wire will also have a much longer life than the line installed in the past.[84]

Whether underground or overhead, the Cooperative's distribution system is GVEC's core reason for existence. And all those who have helped build and maintain that system—past and present—take responsibility for making sure that electric power is delivered to members in the most cost efficient and safe manner possible.

"We have the responsibility for making sure the lights stay on and that's not a job we take lightly," said Bobby Christmas.[85]

Line Work Evolution:
Training the Next Generation of Linemen

Linemen in the twenty-first century are as much the heart and soul of GVEC as they were when the system was first being built in 1938. Bobby Christmas pointed out "a lineman is a unique individual. I've personally never met a breed of people who are more committed to serving others than an electric cooperative lineman. They know that people are depending on them every minute, day and night. When the storms roll in and the lights go out, the members are calling in to wonder when the lights are coming back on."

Christmas added that linemen are "a very proud group of people. It gets in your blood. Young men in the training program are bitten by the adrenaline rush of the job and the knowledge they are doing a job 99 percent of the world wants no part of. Linemen are dedicated to their mission and their brotherhood. Safety is supreme, and the only way one can make a fifty-year career out of it is if he relies on his brother."[86]

GVEC has long recognized the value that competent linemen bring to the Cooperative and its members. When the Texas Electric Cooperatives association (TEC) made the decision to hand over its linemen-training program in 2001, GVEC stepped up to the

As line work continues to grow more complex, the job of a GVEC lineman will follow suit. In a physically and mentally challenging, adrenaline-pumped career, the next generation will enter a field where advancing technologies drive constant change, yet the tradition of safety remains forever paramount.

Former GVEC Line Superintendent Thomas A. Coor, standing left of General Manager Doyle Hines, became the namesake for GVEC's lineman training facility due to his great loyalty and passion for the craft of line work.

plate. With the blessing of General Manager Marcus Pridgeon and the Board of Directors, Bobby Christmas negotiated an agreement with Larry Baker of TEC to build a lineman training center in Gonzales. The facility was named the Thomas A. Coor Lineman Training Facility after the longtime GVEC line superintendent with a passion and loyalty for the craft of line work.

The center opened in 2002 as an overhead field and added an underground field in 2004. Every year, 250 to 300 linemen use the facility, which is one of only two such facilities in the state capable of training linemen for both overhead and underground work. Attendees come from electric cooperatives and municipal electric utilities across the Lone Star State.

With its emphasis on training, GVEC also has been a driving force in the evolution of the Texas Lineman's Rodeo, which invites friendly competition among linemen to strengthen safety, communication, and line work skills. GVEC joined with TEC to spearhead the Rodeo, which was held in San Antonio from 1996 to 2004. TEC decided to drop its sponsorship following the 2004 Rodeo, and GVEC immediately helped form the Texas Lineman's Rodeo Association (TLRA), which moved the competition to Nolte Island in Seguin in 2005 and continues to be hosted at this location today. GVEC is also a sponsor and competitor at the International Lineman's Rodeo, held each October in Bonner Springs, Kansas.

GVEC has always taken seriously its responsibility to keep the lights on. From planning to financing, opening support facilities, responding to new opportunities, evolving with the times or training the next generation, it is the cooperative way to work in the best interest of their member-owners to provide the most valuable services possible.

GVEC opened the Thomas A. Coor Lineman Training Facility in 2002 with overhead training lines and added underground lines in 2004. The facility, located in Gonzales, is one of only two in Texas equipped to train on both technologies.

As a founding member of the Texas Lineman's Rodeo Association, GVEC encourages its linemen and apprentices to participate in the friendly competition against other cooperative and municipal line workers as a way to continually strengthen safety, communication, and job skills.

75 Years of Milestones:
A Chronological Look
Leaders Who Surpass Boundaries

GENERAL MANAGERS

E. A. Hassman
1944-1952

O. W. Davis
1952-1972

Milton "Doyle" Hines
1972-1993

Marcus Pridgeon
1993-2003

Darren Schauer
2003-current

BOARD PRESIDENTS

Milton Lindemann
1938-1959

Monroe Schauer
1959-1986

Lewis Borgfeld
1986-Current

COOPERATIVE FORMED
1938

Led and encouraged by Milton D. Lindemann, GVEC's founding group met in Cost, Texas. As a result of the Texas Cooperative Act, they received a charter to form a cooperative for a $10 fee and created the first Board of Directors. They, along with community volunteers, began signing up members for a $5 membership fee.

LINE CONSTRUCTION BEGINS
1939

The Rural Electrification Administration approves GVEC's first loan of $166,000 in April to build the first distribution lines. Construction began in September.

FIRST LINES ENERGIZED
1940

The first lines were energized in January—servicing about 150 farmers in the Monthalia-Bebe area of Gonzales County. By March, the co-op had built 225 miles of line serving 360 consumers.

ELECTRIC BROODING
1941

Farming sees benefits of electricity with the co-op purchasing and placing a number of brooders on the lines to demonstrate the advantages of using electric heat in poultry houses.

Building Or Remodeling?
THE MODERN HOME IS
ALL-ELECTRIC
Review These Homes

Ask Us About The GVEC
ALL-ELECTRIC
PROGRAM

ALL-ELECTRIC HOMES
1955

GVEC begins promoting all-electric homes to help balance the year-round electric load. This helps keep electricity more affordable as an increasing number of members enjoy the comforts it provides.

APPLIANCE SERVICE & REPAIR SHOP
1968

GVEC opens the Appliance Service and Repair Shop to assist members who were having problems convincing repairmen to travel to their rural homes.

Appliance Service And Repair Shop Open

ESTABLISHED LOCATIONS

1938: Cost Headquarters Established

1948: Seguin South River Street Office Opens
April 1948

1949 : Headquarters Moved to St. Paul Street in Gonzales
December 1949

1956: Seguin Kingsbury Street Office Opens
June 1956

1965: Gonzales Sarah DeWitt Headquarters Opens
June 1965

1968: Schertz 900 Curtiss Avenue Office Opens
July 1968

1999: Schertz 908 Curtiss Avenue Office Opens
March 1999

2001: 24/7, 365 Cooperative Control Center Opens
May 2001

2002: Cuero Office Opens
January 2002

2002: Thomas A. Coor Lineman Training Facility Opens
December 2002

2005: La Vernia Office Opens
October 2005

2009: Seguin Highway 46 Office Opens
April 2009

2011: Western Operations Center Opens
June 2011

OTHER HISTORICAL EVENTS

PURCHASED SCHERTZ AREA LINES FROM SAN ANTONIO
April 1948
1948

FIRST CAPITAL CREDITS RETIRED AND PAID TO MEMBERS
December 1955
1955

GVEC INTRODUCES SEVERAL PROGRAMS TO SAVE ENERGY
January–December 1973
1973

20-YEAR POWER CONTRACT WITH GBRA TAKES EFFECT
January 1980
1980

GVEC IMPLEMENTS NEW STRATEGIC PLANNING PROCESS
January 2004
2004

GVEC FIRST TO PAY OFF REA LOAN

1986

GVEC is the first electric cooperative in the nation to pay off its REA loan. The co-op receives instant equity by paying a discounted amount while gaining new opportunities for financing and flexibility in operations.

GVDC IS FORMED

1987

Understanding the role rural infrastructure plays in economic vitality and stability, the Guadalupe Valley Development Corporation is formed as a nonprofit subsidiary to provide loans to public service organizations such as rural water supply corporations and volunteer fire departments and to help with the development of area industrial parks.

GVEC OFFERS RURAL TV

1988

TV programming is limited, leading to the creation of the Guadalupe Valley Satellite Communications (Rural TV) to provide more options for members.

GVEC HOME IS ESTABLISHED

1998

Members appreciated the service the GVEC Appliance Service & Repair Shop provided; the shop was expanded in June, becoming GVEC Home Services, Inc. It offered a broader range of services including sales and service of heating and cooling systems, water heaters and brand-name appliances. Today there are three GVEC Home stores in Gonzales, La Vernia and Seguin.

GVEC.NET OFFERS INTERNET

1998

Many members living in the GVEC territory couldn't find stable Internet service that offered local access to the Web without high long-distance charges. With a strong commitment to enhancing members' lives, GVEC created GVEC.net which provided a reliable connection that was also more affordable.

GVEC MERGES WITH DEWITT

2002

GVEC consolidates with DeWitt Electric Cooperative, adding to GVEC's service territory and membership. The merger results in an economy of scale that helps keep service affordable for all.

WHOLESALE POWER

2010

The GVEC Board decides not to renew its restrictive and long-term, all-requirements wholesale power contract with LCRA which ends in 2016. After intensive study, it was determined the move to more diversified and competitively priced sources would provide the flexibility needed to address future industry and political challenges in our mission of keeping electricity affordable.

GVEC TURNS 75

2013

The Cooperative continues to grow and now serves members with 8,068 overhead and 513 underground miles of distribution line and 229 miles of transmission line. GVEC provides service to over 71,100 consumers and serves one of the largest clusters of commercial and industrial-based customers in the region.

GVEC staff, directors, and guests celebrated the grand opening of the Western Operations Center (WOC) located at 6400 IH-10 West in Seguin in 2011. The Center was a result of a twenty-year projection of significant population and meter growth in Guadalupe and Wilson Counties by 2025.

Chapter **Five**

The Impact of TECHNOLOGY

Over its seventy-five-year history, technology has been one of the most important drivers of operational efficiencies and expanding member services. Affecting every area of the Cooperative from constructing lines, to billing, communications, monitoring and more—GVEC would not be able to deliver effective and reliable service today without implementing new technologies when and where it benefits the membership.

GVEC has long been a firm believer in the philosophy of leading the way for its members and industry. That streak of initiative and self-sufficiency dates back to the earliest days of the Cooperative, when farmer members rolled up their sleeves and brought electric power to rural South Central Texas. The electric cooperative built simply to supply electricity to the country farms has evolved into a multifaceted resource for its member-owners; a result of coupling hard work with advanced technologies when and where they make sense.

Much of the technological advances of the past quarter-century has been driven by computerization. GVEC was an early adopter of computer technology for the simple reason that member meters had to be read each month, and then compiled into monthly bills that were sent to the member. Over the years, the Cooperative's use of technology has grown and can be seen today in virtually every aspect of GVEC services.

Hand-Billing Everything

In the early days of the Cooperative, members themselves read the meters and filled out a record of their reading. And at a time when neighborliness dictated a visit to town once or twice a week, many members paid their monthly bills in person. Retired employees Leon Netardus and Betty Nell DuPree remember well the laborious tasks associated with billing thousands of accounts by hand.

Leon Netardus came to work for GVEC in 1954 and held the position of business manager among other roles for GVEC.

When Leon Netardus came to work at GVEC's old building on Saint Paul Street in Gonzales in December 1954, the Cooperative was just catching its breath after eight years of breakneck expansion following the end of World War II. A Gonzales High School graduate and U.S. Army veteran, Netardus recalled just how little of the Cooperative's operations were automated back then.

"We had eight thousand accounts in 1954," he said, "and we were hand-billing everything."[87] Betty Nell DuPree, a Belton native who was hired as a temporary employee to help with the distribution of capital credits in 1959, recalled typing lists with a Royal upright typewriter. Copies were made with carbon paper and onionskin paper, and in the days before "Wite-out," a mistake meant ripping the paper out of the typewriter and starting over.[88]

Twice-monthly billings involved transferring account information from Boston Ledgers, adding totals with a hand-cranked Burroughs Accounting Machine, typing up bills, running envelopes with a foot-operated metal stencil machine, and hand-stuffing the bills into the envelopes.

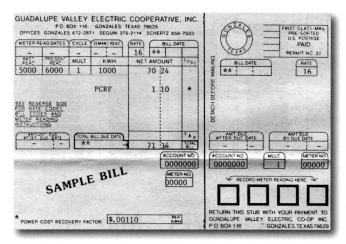

In order to cut expenses for the Co-op, the Board of Directors switched from hand billing within two billing periods per month to postcard billing in one period in 1966.

In 1966, the Board of Directors changed from two billing periods per month to one and switched to postcard billing in order to cut billing expenses for the Co-op.

When Leon Netardus retired as GVEC's business manager thirty-eight years later in 1992, he had experienced a full transition from hand-billing everything to a full fledge technologically sophisticated cooperative. It all started with the use of punch cards.

Billing: Using Punch Cards

In the 1950s and 1960s, when GVEC first stuck its toe in the computerization waters, the correct term was data processing. GVEC, like most utilities, had a mass of data that needed to be processed each month in the form of bills, accounts receivable, accounts payable, and bank deposits. As late as the 1970s, GVEC had accounts at fifteen separate banks in the territory. Back office personnel had to keep track of all of those customer and banking accounts.

The first computers, based on models introduced by IBM in the 1950s, used punch cards to process data. Key-punch operators, so called because they manually entered data into the computer, which then recorded the information on punch cards, were an integral part of the system. Once recorded, the punch cards could store and print out billing and account information.

Accounting employees including Betty Nell DuPree and Betty Jo Shanklin rejoiced when GVEC took delivery of its first IBM computer in 1963 utilizing a punch card system: the Co-op's first step toward automatic data processing.

When GVEC took delivery of its first IBM computer in 1963, Betty Nell DuPree and her colleagues in billing and accounting rejoiced. The punch card system was a big step forward toward automatic data processing.

Although seemingly archaic to a generation that has grown up with computers, punch cards were a major technologic leap forward for GVEC and other companies that needed to convert to automatic data processing for back office operations.

Billing: A Technological Revolution

As the first at GVEC to work with computers, it was only natural that staff should suggest they advance to the next step of programming the computers for the Cooperative's billing needs. Betty Nell DuPree and Betty Jo Shanklin attended programming school in Dallas at the IBM offices and returned to Gonzales to show others in the Billing Department how to program. Since the mid-1970s, the in-house programming staff was handling all of the programming for billing and even getting involved in programming for the Rate Department.[89] The in-house programmers also were able to convert the system from once-a-month billing to cycle billing in November 1986, in which a quarter of the Cooperative's bills went out every week.[90]

As the Cooperative grew, the rate of changes in technologies grew even more rapidly and GVEC essentially outgrew its capacity to handle the demand internally. The Cooperative decided in 1997 to hire a national data processing firm to handle programming the system, freeing up the Billing Department to reconcile automated meter reading, another of the technological advances stemming from the implementation of computers.

When data programming demands exceeded GVEC's internal capacity in 1997, Data Processing Supervisor Mary Ellen Shelton led the conversion to outsource needs to Southeastern Data Cooperative (SEDC); a major transformation which automated GVEC data processing.

The conversion was led by the team of Darren Schauer, then manager of the Computer Information Services Division established by General Manager Marcus Pridgeon in 1997; and Mary Ellen Shelton, then supervisor of Data Processing. It was handled by Southeastern Data Cooperative (SEDC) of Atlanta, Georgia, and involved a comprehensive, system-wide change. Staff had to relearn everything they knew about data processing, and routines developed over decades were totally changed. "It was a lot of blood and tears" for the eight people in the Billing Department in Gonzales and their counterparts in Seguin and Schertz, DuPree said. "We had to adjust to it, but when it was done, it was wonderful."[91] Schauer recalled the transition of the billing and accounting system to SEDC as a major transformation. "It restructured how we interacted with our customers," he said. "We now had a linked network between all offices. This pushed the various responsibilities of doing business out to each office as opposed to having the entire load of data processing centralized in Gonzales. We were also able to implement a new paper bill in October 2005 with auto-populated information foregoing the need for postcard billing. GVEC had become more automated and efficient than ever before."[92]

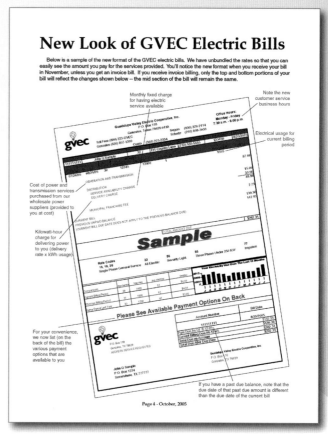

New Look of GVEC Electric Bills

Below is a sample of the new format of the GVEC electric bills. We have unbundled the rates so that you can easily see the amount you pay for the services provided. You'll notice the new format when you receive your bill in November, unless you get an invoice bill. If you receive invoice billing, only the top and bottom portions of your bill will reflect the changes shown below -- the mid section of the bill will remain the same.

Page 4 - October, 2005

GVEC introduced paper billing in October 2005 due to the enhanced capability of SEDC to auto-populate account information and unbundle billing rates so members could easily see the amount they were paying for service.

The responsibilities of daily business were shared by customer service representatives in Seguin, Schertz, and Gonzales as a result of the new automated billing and accounting system and linked network. GVEC became more efficient than ever before for its membership. Shown above is former CSR Shirley Boedeker.

In 2001, GVEC opened its state-of-the-art twenty-four-hour, 365-day manned Cooperative Control Center (CCC) in Gonzales. The CCC houses the SCADA system and continues to serve today as the dispatch hub for on-call crews as well as the epicenter of remote line repair and monitoring.

Working under then General Manager Doyle Hines, Engineering Division Manager Steve Slaughter (standing) led the establishment of the Load Management Center in Gonzales and implemented the Cooperative's Supervisory Control and Data Acquisition system in 1984. This gave GVEC its first capabilities to remotely control and monitor the electric distribution system.

The computerization of GVEC's billing and accounting system, which began with punch cards in the 1960s and set the stage for desktop computer implementation in the late 1980s and 1990s, led to a technological revolution of the way the Cooperative does business in every facet. And that revolution has continued unabated for the better part of two decades now.

Changes in System Monitoring and Metering

Some at the Cooperative would say no area has experienced greater changes over the past seventy-five years than that of line monitoring and metering. Perhaps this is true considering GVEC planted its roots with and ran for many years through pure physical labor, but has expanded over time into a technology-rich organization.

One of the most remarkable advances in the technological history of GVEC occurred in 1984 under the leadership of General Manager Doyle Hines with the assistance of Engineering Division Manager Steve Slaughter. The Cooperative established its Load Management Center in the Gonzales office and implemented a Supervisory Control and Data Acquisition (SCADA) system: a progressive move at the time. This gave GVEC operations the ability to remotely control power to selected appliances in members' homes as part of the Volunteer to Improve Power Use (VIP) load management program started in 1982 (see more in Chapter 6). Over the next decade plus, the sophistication of the SCADA technology developed into a critical tool used to monitor and control the GVEC electric distribution and transmission system.

The opening of a twenty-four-hour-a-day manned, state-of-the-art Cooperative Control Center (CCC) in Gonzales in 2001 allowed operations personnel the first opportunity to dispatch on-call service linemen around the clock in each area of the Cooperative's service territory, ensuring quick response in the event of an outage.[93] Gone were the days of a single employee dispatching from other facilities and linemen physically driving to different locations to identify and address every issue. The Cooperative became much more efficient in communication and logistics with the use of the SCADA system combined with Geographic Information Systems (GIS) technology, and this opened the door to further advances including automated meter reading (AMR) and outage prediction capabilities.

Monitoring and Metering Changes: From GIS to AMR

In 1995, GVEC began to automate its mapping system. Since the establishment of the Cooperative in 1938, GVEC's draftsman had been drawing all maps, work orders, and staking sheets by hand. By the mid-1990s, GVEC had grown to more than thirty-three thousand members, and maintaining a mapping system manually was increasingly difficult.

Bobby O'Neal, who began as a draftsman for the Cooperative in 1979, said draftsmen drew all the drawings for the line crews. A staking sheet in the 1980s typically required about twenty-five copies, which were run off on a mimeograph machine. If the staking sheet was on white paper, it was for work in the Gonzales area; if it was on yellow paper, the job was in the Seguin area. "But it was still purple ink from the mimeograph," he said.[94]

In 1996, GVEC became one of the nation's first rural electric cooperatives to adopt Geographic Information System (GIS) mapping that used satellites to locate

For many years, draftsmen prepared drawings by hand and steadily moved into computerization. In 1996, GVEC became one of the nation's first cooperatives to adopt Geographic Information Systems (GIS) mapping for faster response to trouble calls.

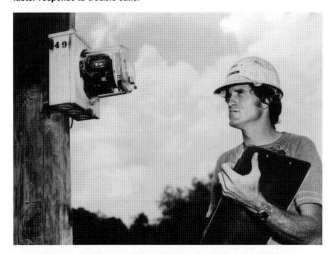

Retired Engineering Manager Bobby O'Neal, who started with GVEC as a Meter Tech in the late 1970s, worked for the Cooperative from the manual drafting process all the way through to complete automation incorporating GIS as well as automated meter reading.

Automated meter reading (AMR) technology was implemented in 2002 and eliminated the need for GVEC members to read their own meters; a practice which had been in place since the Cooperative's inception.

the longitudinal and latitudinal coordinates of GVEC's electric facilities, in some cases down to individual distribution poles. Marcus Pridgeon explained that with the new technology, "GVEC will be able to respond to trouble calls in a much more efficient and prompt manner."[95]

GVEC welcomed the new millennium with a technological milestone of another sort when it began installing meters throughout the territory that were read electronically from the GVEC office in 2002. Automated meter reading (AMR), also known as "smart meters" due to their ability to be read remotely, finally eliminated one of the more cumbersome throwbacks to the Cooperative's roots. No longer would members have to read their own meters and send those readings into the GVEC office. With AMR, the former practice was relegated to the past. The Cooperative instantly became more efficient and it was able to enter the twenty-first century both figuratively and literally.

Technology Drives Improvement in Outage Response

GIS and AMR meters signified a change in not only the process of locating accounts and meter reading, but also the process of outage reporting. The technology allowed GVEC to introduce its Automated Outage Reporting System in 2002. In the case of an outage, members were now able to call in their number to an automated system that quickly and seamlessly scheduled the meter for restoration of service.[96] The automated system used telephone numbers, account numbers, or meter numbers to identify each meter on the system.

The efficient use of technology allowed GVEC to better benchmark statistics in a number of outage management categories. By 2008, the Cooperative was meeting benchmarks for customer average interruption duration (how long a member is out of power), and exceeding them for system average interruption duration (overall how long members are out of power during the year) and system average interruption frequency (overall how many times are members out of power).[98]

As the Cooperative approached its seventy-fifth anniversary, GVEC worked to make state-of-the-art technology upgrades. In 2008 and 2009, crews completed the installation of a fiber optic network between all GVEC substations from Gonzales to San Antonio, making it easier to communicate with new technologies that helped to monitor and control the Cooperative's system. GVEC also upgraded its GIS mapping and telephone systems to allow dispatchers and line crews to respond even faster during outages.[99]

A new Western Operations Center (WOC) broke ground in Seguin in the spring of 2010 and opened a little over a year later. Equipped with the most modern technology, the WOC was a reaction to GVEC's twenty-year projection of population and meter growth, showing membership growth could double by 2025, with most of that growth taking place in Guadalupe and Wilson Counties.

A Moment In Time:
Outage Reporting Before Automation

For the first forty-plus years of GVEC service, reporting outages and monitoring the lines during inclement weather was largely dependent upon notifications from the membership. Showing concern for personal needs, in case of weather-related outages during thunder and lightning storms, members were asked to place a collect telephone call to the Cooperative's offices in Gonzales and later Seguin was also included. In May 1954, General Manager O. W. Davis told members that the volume of collect calls typically gave dispatchers a good idea where the lines were down or out during business hours.

Ronnie Foreman, who started as a lineman with GVEC in 1966, recalls, "Although they didn't work for GVEC, the wives unofficially served as 'after hours' dispatchers when their husbands were on call." Back then, the names and home phone numbers of service linemen were printed in the monthly newsletter [and phone book] and members were directed to phone them after hours to report outages at their home. Foreman adds, "My wife would stay up all night answering calls. I drove to wherever I had a trouble call, and when I'd come back home, she'd tell me I had four more calls to go on. I learned to rely a lot on finding the nearest pay phone." But no matter the time of day or night, Foreman says "it was always a good feeling when you made a member happy by getting their lights back on."

Linemen wives were largely off the hook toward the late 1970s and early 1980s. Outage relaying became the work of the Gonzales County Sheriff's Department and the Guadalupe-Blanco River Authority for Guadalupe County according to former lineman Bobby Christmas. "Members contacted the two agencies and they would then call us by radio or phone, then we went to a pager system. We used this system until 1989 when we began dispatching from the Gonzales office."[97]

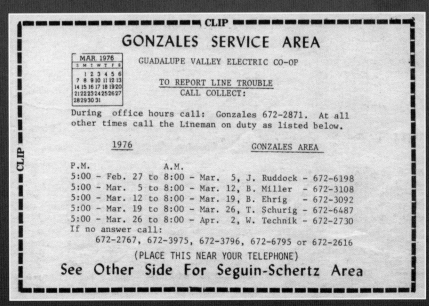

Ads like this were published in the GVEC newsletter, giving members the home phone numbers of on-call linemen to address outages. Until the 1970s, linemen wives unofficially served as after-hours dispatchers directing their husbands to trouble calls when they would check in.

The first of its kind for GVEC, the WOC was Gold Certified in Leadership in Environmental Energy and Design for its sustainable, environmentally-friendly features including recycled construction materials, xeriscaping, and energy conservation based features.

By locating the latest technologies in the heart of that growth area, GVEC could ensure the highest quality of service and lowest operational cost to serve existing and new members in the area.[100] The new center enabled GVEC to enhance data integrity by providing redundancy for the CCC's SCADA system in Gonzales. In addition to the functionality, the WOC obtained Gold certification in Leadership in Environmental Energy and Design (LEED) for its sustainable, environmentally friendly features such as eco-friendly construction materials and xeriscaping with native plants among many others. The facility was also equipped with solar water heating, a set of solar voltaic panels and a wind turbine to offset energy usage along with a rainwater harvester for watering the landscaping. Each of these features serve the functionality of the facility as well as educate local students and civic organizations on renewable energy and water conservation.

The willingness to make the capital investments in new technology and state-of-the art facilities such as the Western Operations Center as necessary to better serve members has been a hallmark of GVEC's core philosophy for three-quarters-of-a-century. Members today will likely not even recognize the technological innovations that will drive the Cooperative seventy-five years from now.

The Role of Technology Today

Today, technology also is playing a major role in allowing members to closely monitor all of their interactions with GVEC. In 2010, the Cooperative introduced its on-line customer Self-Service Portal, which allowed members for the first time to view their bill in real-time on-line, update their address and phone number, access the previous twenty-four months of statements, sign up for text or e-mail bill alerts, and apply for disconnection of existing service or for new service.[101]

GVEC continued to beef up its on-line customer service presence in 2010–2011, adding e-bill and on-line payments, interactive voice response (IVR) messaging, postcards and letter notifications of operations projects, outage viewing via an interactive map on gvec.org, and on-line chat capability with customer service representatives. The main driver behind the decision to offer members the ability to do business online came from the members themselves. GVEC had conducted a member survey in 2010 in which members said they wanted it to be convenient and easy to do business with the Cooperative at any time as well as stay informed of activities. With this in mind, GVEC continues to improve communication with multiple ways in which to meet the new and evolving needs of its member-owners.

As the cooperative advances, it continues to invest in technology to bring services to members in the most efficient measure as possible. The overall efficiency of GVEC today is very much dependent upon technology. This is an aspect of the Cooperative that will grow exponentially as GVEC continues to expand in members, meters, and diverse services.

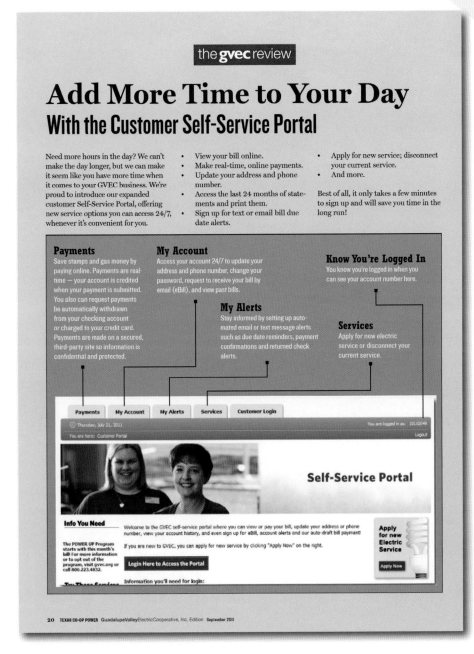

Responding to the growing use of technology by the late 2000s, GVEC was steadily introducing online tools and services to make doing business with the Co-op easy. In 2010, GVEC launched its first online Customer Service Portal on www.gvec.org, allowing members to access account information and pay their electric bill at their personal convenience.

For generations, local second graders have come to know and love Louie the Lightning Bug, GVEC's mascot for electrical safety.

Chapter **Six**

Member Services That
MAKE A DIFFERENCE

The unique business model of a cooperative is centered on member service. Though erecting poles and wires and delivering reliable and affordable electricity is an integral aspect of service, GVEC member services extend beyond lines to encourage efficiency, inspire education and safety, and support community needs.

The immense job of providing electric power to residents of GVEC's service territory in the years following World War II left little room for Cooperative employees to focus on anything else. But from the start of the Cooperative, member services had been a primary focus of GVEC. Without the members, GVEC would not exist. Everybody at the Cooperative offices and on the line crews serving the area understood that fact.

In 1953, GVEC instituted an essential component of its member services program that exists to this day. The Cooperative established a member services newspaper to keep folks informed of what the Cooperative was doing and to provide information on how to live better electrically to rural residents of Gonzales, Guadalupe, Lavaca, and Wilson Counties. GVEC noted that the new publication, called *Co-op News and Views*, would carry "news of interest to you as a member of the Co-op that will bring you information on new and improved power uses that will be entertaining and instructive."[102]

Willie Wiredhand, an icon of the rural electrification movement, would make his first appearance in *Co-op News and Views* in the June 1953 issue, reminding members "electric energy is the most economical and efficient servant in your home."[103] Over the next few years, the newsletter's name would change to the *Information Bulletin*.

In the 1950s and the 1960s, the Cooperative used its *Information Bulletin* to keep members current with the latest developments in electric energy for the farm

and home. In September 1957, members who raised poultry found of great interest an article on how electric brooders could increase profits. Member Otto Kuntschik of Harwood reported the electric brooder for his fifty-four-hundred-bird capacity broiler house used just over a fraction of one-fourth cent per bird for electric energy per year.[104]

Willie Wiredhand, an icon of the rural electrification movement, made his first appearance with GVEC in the the 1950s monthly newsletter entitled *Co-op News and Views* and was used to promote the use of electricity and the benefits of becoming a co-op member owner.

Ads encouraging the increased use of electricity regularly appeared in the second edition of the GVEC monthly newsletter published in the 1950s and 1960s entitled the *Information Bulletin*.

From the 1960s to the 1970s, members received information through *Texas Co-op Power* magazine. In 1974, GVEC introduced *The GVEC Review*, produced cover to cover by internal staff, which remained in use for the next thirty-five years.

For the farm home, the *Information Bulletin* also introduced members to the latest in modern appliance conveniences, including electric dryers and electric blankets. Under the direction of General Managers O. W. Davis and Doyle Hines, the Cooperative worked diligently to acquaint members with the benefits of electric heat, electric air conditioning, and the all-electric home.

From the mid-1960s, members were kept informed of the many changes occurring in cooperative business as well as member services and energy efficiency through a subscription to *Texas Co-op Power* magazine produced jointly by the statewide association of Texas Electric Cooperatives and GVEC until January 1974. At this point, the Cooperative was in a position to publish their own individual newsletter introduced as *The GVEC Review*. The new publication would be produced cover to cover by GVEC staff and included news and information regarding GVEC business and the electric industry. Stories on local people, places, and events in the GVEC service territory and family recipes submitted by members, which had become a cooperative member tradition by this time, were featured within the newsletter.

This stand-alone publication would be in place through January of 2009 at which point *The GVEC Review* was incorporated within *Texas Co-op Power* magazine once again for distribution to members. The

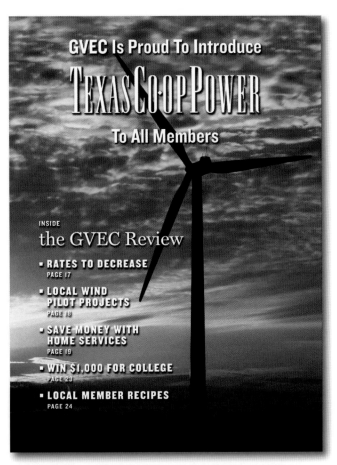

In January 2009, *The GVEC Review* was incorporated into the newly revitalized *Texas Co-op Power* magazine. The magazine, which mixed local people and places with statewide energy-related topics, was the preferred source of news and information from GVEC in a 2012 member communications survey.

Public relations efforts to communicate the value of rural electrification spurred visits to Home Economics Departments in area schools to teach the wise use of electricity to the children of members. From the 1950s through today, GVEC has offered youth programs based on safety, energy efficiency, leadership, and higher learning as part of its member services.

newly revitalized magazine offered members more information on the energy industry than ever before combined with the local flavor articles members had become accustomed to over the years. By 2013, GVEC members, through communication surveys, had identified *Texas Co-op Power* magazine as their number one preferred source of news and information updates from GVEC.

The Member Services Division

Up until the 1960s, the job of making sure that members were comfortable with electricity in their homes and on their farms was divided up between the power use advisor and the public relations advisor.[105] Both positions were highly involved with member services. Doyle Hines, who began his

career with GVEC in 1958 as the power use advisor, worked closely with members to ensure that they were using electric energy as wisely and efficiently as possible around their farms. Leon Netardus was named to the newly created position of public relations advisor in 1957 "to fill a growing need for increased activity in member and public relations and informational services."[106]

Public relations was necessary because GVEC and other cooperatives like it represented a competitive threat to the investor-owned utilities that had developed markets in the early years of the century. While GVEC's relations with entities such as Central Power & Light Company in Corpus Christi were generally positive, other rural electric cooperatives in parts of Texas and nationwide had a much more contentious relationship with investor-owned utility neighbors. GVEC participated in advertising campaigns sponsored by the National Rural Electric Cooperative Association (NRECA) that reminded members of the services rural electric cooperatives provided. But GVEC's main focus was on demonstrating to its members the value of rural electrification.

Over the years, many talented individuals have established new channels of communication with the GVEC membership. Among the ranks of leading Cooperative writers, photographers, and public relations professionals are Clarence Hallmark (pictured), Leon Netardus, and Barbara Kuck.

The Member Services Division, which grew out of the Cooperative's public relations initiatives of the 1950s and was formally established in January 1967, began diversifying its efforts in the late 1960s. During the 1960s, GVEC would hold power use promotions in cooperation with local appliance dealers, but by mid-decade it had become apparent that members were having difficulties in getting major appliances repaired and serviced once they were purchased. Accordingly, GVEC first established the appliance service and repair shop in July of 1968; then in 1977, the Cooperative assigned full-time appliance repairmen to the Schertz and Seguin areas.

Perhaps the best-known Member Services initiative over the years was the *GVEC Trading Post*, which was started by Leon Netardus and the Public Relations Division in December 1957. The popular radio show, which aired on KCTI in Gonzales, KWED in Seguin, and KRJH in Hallettsville let members and nonmembers place classified advertisements at no charge. The *Trading Post* also carried announcements of local events and items of Cooperative interest to GVEC members. Along with an online version introduced in 2009 on the Cooperative's website, the *Trading Post* continued to run on KCTI 1460 in Gonzales as of 2013.

Member Information Committees

In the 1970s and 1980s, the Member Services Division took on a new task under the direction of Member Services Manager John Fritz. The energy crises of 1973 and 1979, coupled with rampant inflation in the early 1980s upended the economy of scale model for utilities that had previously meant the more kilowatt-hours consumed, the cheaper each kilowatt hour became. GVEC, like most utilities across the nation, had kept members informed of how they could use energy wisely and efficiently, holding down monthly costs during the process.

Double-digit inflation and spiraling interest rates that reached 15 percent in 1981 plagued the economy from 1978 to 1985. Electric utilities, which were particularly capital intensive, were especially susceptible to high

One way in which the Cooperative exhibited that value was through providing benefits to the children of members. As early as the 1950s, GVEC participated with local schools in sponsoring 4-H programs and a driver's education safety course.[107] In the 1960s and 1970s, GVEC cooperated with the Home Economics Departments of area schools in a program to teach the wise use of electricity; the Cooperative placed electric ranges, freezers, washers, and dryers in sixteen schools in the area. Other popular youth programs were "Food Fun for Juniors" in which a home economics expert trained in Co-op principles provided cooking classes for girls in local schools; and the Government in Action Youth Tour, which allowed local high schools students the opportunity to travel to Washington, D.C.[108]

Member Services Manager John Fritz was instrumental in the formation of Member Information Committees from the 1970s through the late 2000s to help GVEC explain to other members how the Cooperative was handling issues such as rate increases and other business.

interest rates and out-of-control inflation since they had to borrow money to build power plants and transmission lines to serve growing demand. As a result of the financial upheavals of the period, GVEC and other electric utilities were forced to raise electric rates to combat inflation and high interest rates.

GVEC worked hard to mitigate the impact of rate increases by communicating to members how best to conserve energy—and reduce monthly bills. The Cooperative became a leader in load management initiatives due to its good relations with members. In 1975, GVEC had established member information committees in each district to ensure that the owners of the Cooperative were fully informed on GVEC's problems, objectives, and accomplishments. Made up of couples from each of GVEC's nine districts, the membership committee met twice a year to review home weatherization issues, load management, and LCRA's attempts to meet demand by building the coal-fired Fayette units.

GVEC's attempts to keep the membership informed included a series of public meetings held during the 1980s to discuss rate increase requests. When tempers at the meetings got heated, GVEC Board members and staff could count on the member information committee to advocate to other members and explain steps the Cooperative was taking to lessen the impact of rate increases.

Committees Lead to New Services

Working with the Member Information Committees in the 1970s and 1980s, Doyle Hines, and by the late 1970s the team of Hines and Fritz, created a number

of innovative load management programs that helped customers manage their monthly electric use, cut electric bills and established the Cooperative as a leader in shaving peak demand to keep wholesale power costs at a minimum. GVEC's first foray into energy conservation was its home insulation program in 1973. That led to other innovative programs. GVEC launched the Home Energy Audit Program (HEAP) in the Schertz area as early as 1978. Three years later, in 1981, the Conservation Plan 5 program was added to help finance energy efficiency improvements to member homes. The plan offered loans ranging from $1,000 to $5,000, based on the size of apartment or home, for up to five years and 5 percent interest. In 1982, GVEC offered the Volunteer to Improve Power Use (VIP) program in which members could volunteer to withhold electricity usage during peak times.

GVEC launched a comprehensive load management program in 1984 to help trim electricity usage during periods of peak use. Called Peak Time Intermission (PTI), the program involved the transmission of a signal to a member's home to cycle electric heating and air conditioning. The program worked to ensure that all of the cooling, heating, and water heating

GVEC offered energy efficiency services such as the Home Energy Audit Program as early as the 1970s to educate members on how to increase efficiency within their homes and businesses.

To help trim peak time kilowatt usage during the 1980s, GVEC offered the Peak Time Intermission Program in which members volunteered to install load control devices on air conditioning, heating, and water heaters which GVEC could cycle off remotely if necessary. Clint Petras installed the ten thousandth device in 1990 and the program would go on to include twenty thousand devices.

units on the Cooperative's system did not come on at the same time, thereby leveling out peak demand in both winter and summer. The intermission times were seldom long enough to cause any discomfort or problems for the homeowner.

PTI started as a volunteer program and quickly caught on. In September 1990, then GVEC Load Control Technician Clint Petras installed the ten-thousandth-load control device at the home of retiree Arthur McElroy and his wife, Grace, in Hallettsville.[109] The program would go on to consist of nearly twenty thousand devices and would allow GVEC to manage peak loads in both winter and summer.

The Good Cents Home

In the early 1990s, GVEC began to promote building energy efficient homes through participation in the Lower Colorado River Authority's Good Cents Home Program. Through the program, GVEC member

services advisors would guide members and builders through the stringent process of qualifying for the certification. Members were quick to recognize the value in lower electric bills by implementing such features as ample wall, flooring, and attic insulation, window and door caulking, moisture and infiltration barriers, attic ventilation, and the installation of an energy saving electric heat pump as well as other features. GVEC also offered specific rebates in association with the program as incentive for participation. By 1993, early adopters of the program began receiving certificates verifying their new home would not only save them money on future electric bills, but also increase the overall value of the home. The certificate came with a "Good Cents" home sign proudly displaying the home was built to the highest efficiency standards of the time.

The Value of Energy Audits

The Cooperative's early efficiency research had determined that there were a number of energy wasters that could be easily identified and rectified for members. The top energy wasters included leaky heating and cooling ductwork; refrigerators and freezers with damaged seals and dirty coils; swimming pools lacking timers to cycle off pump motors; hot water heaters without a timer on the circulating pumps; lack of insulation; oversized attic fans and inadequate attic ventilation; and dirty air filters.[110] To combat these issues, GVEC introduced complimentary energy audits to its members.

Member services advisors have been conducting complimentary energy audits in the homes of GVEC members since 1978; a service which continues through today.

In an audit, an experienced energy expert, such as Robert Frederick, conducts a full investigation of the home checking for items such as adequate insulation as well as the age and condition of air conditioning and heating sources among a host of other items.

GVEC's Home Energy Checkup has been offered free to members since 1978. As part of the program, a trained member services advisor visits the member's home or place of business and evaluates the property's energy efficiency, paying particular attention to adequate insulation and ventilation, heating, cooling and hot water heating systems, lighting efficiency, leakage around doors, windows, skylights, and electrical openings, and the efficiency of home energy appliances.[111]

Once the audit is complete, the member services advisor provides the member-owner with a detailed report, indicating problem areas along with a list of recommendations explaining what steps can be taken to reduce energy costs. GVEC's energy expert will discuss how an individual family's lifestyle can impact energy usage and overall monthly energy bill and answer any questions members might have.[112]

Advisors have incorporated the use of a thermal imaging camera utilizing infrared technology to seek out various temperature changes in the home, identifying the largest sources of energy waste. The darker colors indicate where cool air is escaping in this air-conditioning duct photo.

Over the years, home energy audits have become more technologically sophisticated since their introduction in 1978. Today's member services advisors implement the capabilities of a thermal imaging (IR) camera that utilizes infrared technology to detect potential problems hidden behind walls that may be contributing to wasted energy. It does this by measuring the temperature differences of an object (like a wall) and then transforming the data into a colorful thermal image that GVEC's efficiency experts are trained to interpret.[113]

Introduced in 2012, the IR cameras joined other high-technology tools that made energy audits even more meaningful. The Home Energy Suite, a collection of free, on-line energy efficiency tools, helped members monitor their energy lifestyle with energy calculators, a do-it-yourself home audit, and an interactive energy library. Just for the GVEC mini-members, Kids Korner, accessed on www.gvec.org, offered efficiency, renewable, and safety lessons and games for kids through 2012.

Conservation Plan 7

Electric utility engineers have made a fascinating discovery in the past thirty years. Conserving energy at the point of use pays huge dividends in reduced fuel use. Customers that insulate their homes, use energy-efficient light bulbs and allow their utility to monitor and control energy-intensive appliances like water heaters can cut their electricity bills by 40 to 50 percent or more. And the utility can provide the same reliable service as before with a far lower consumption of fuel, be it coal, natural gas, nuclear or renewable energy.

GVEC and the rural electric cooperative movement have accelerated their commitment to energy conservation in the twenty-first century as coal and natural gas have become more expensive and under increasing attack from the nation's environmental community.

Beginning in 2001, new homes or businesses built had to comply with Texas Energy Codes set by the U.S.

Department of Energy (DOE) and the International Energy Conservation Code (IECC), as well as comply with the Energy Policy Act of 1992. The Codes consisted of minimum energy conservation requirements for windows, wall R-values, ceiling R-values, and other building components.[114]

"The added bonus is that through the energy-conserving modifications, the end result will be lower electric bills."

Recognizing that many of its member-owners lived in or worked out of buildings that were constructed prior to the Texas Energy Codes, GVEC unveiled its Conservation Plan 7 in 2002, the predecessor to the original Conservation Plan 5, to help members get more financing than ever before for energy-efficient improvements to an existing home or business. With the Conservation 7 program, members could secure loans of up to $7,000 to make energy efficiency improvements. The loans required a down payment and sales tax, and the interest rate was 7 percent. Monthly payments were added to the GVEC electric bill, and there was no penalty for prepayment.[115] Loans could be used to insulate windows, doors, attics, and walls; install central electric heat pumps and ductwork; add electric water heaters, heat exchangers, and hot water banks; and install load shedding equipment, energy saving lighting fixtures, and commercial building energy-management systems.

GVEC noted that for member-owners, "the added bonus is that through the energy-conserving modifications, the end result will be lower electric bills."[116]

Energy Efficiency Rebates

GVEC's admirable position of serving a community that was rapidly growing in the second decade of the twenty-first century meant the Cooperative was daily dealing with the construction of new homes and subdivisions across its service territory. To encourage the continued construction of the most energy-efficient homes and businesses possible, GVEC established a complete series of energy efficiency rebates in April 2010. Although this was not the first time in its history the Cooperative had offered rebates, it was the first time they were offered as a whole home approach to efficiency incentives. The rebate program was targeted at new home construction, but also encouraged member-owners to make home improvements to existing properties and install renewable distributive generation in wind and eventually included solar options as well.

The GVEC Energy Efficiency New Home Rebate offered minimum rebates of $2,050 for construction of all-electric homes, and varying allowances for the installation of Energy Star Appliances, energy efficient heat pumps and electric water heaters, as well as the installation of attic and wall insulation and high efficiency windows. Rebates of $1,500 or less were credited to the member's GVEC electric account, while rebates of more than $1,500 were reimbursed by check.[117]

Home improvement rebates were available for cooling and heating heat pump systems, insulation, window replacement, solar screens and films, duct system replacements, and heat pump water heaters. Homeowners were required to use a GVEC-listed contractor to qualify for any of the Cooperative's energy efficiency rebates.

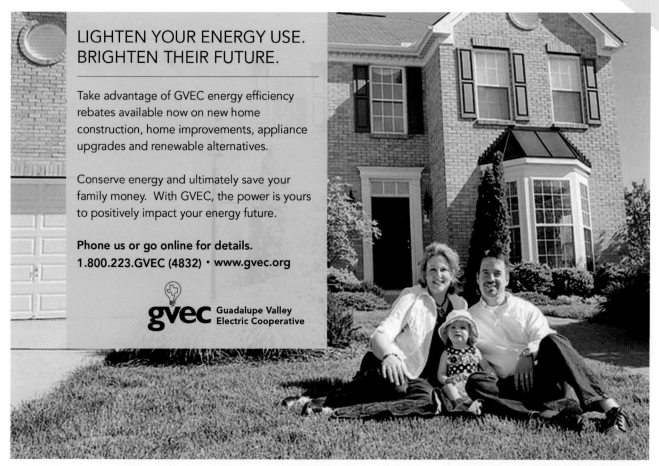

While various rebates have typically been a part of member services, GVEC established a comprehensive rebate program in 2010. Addressing efficiency in the home from appliances to renewable alternatives, the rebate program has gone through some changes, but remains in effect for members to utilize still today.

Homeowners could also capture rebates up to $8,000 for installation of solar photovoltaic systems. Lesser rebates were available for installation of solar water heaters, solar water well pumps, and wind generators.[118]

GVEC supported the energy efficiency rebates with the 2011 establishment of an online rebate center where members could find general information on GVEC rebates for energy efficient new home construction, home improvements, and renewable energy alternatives. Additionally, the rebate center listed GVEC-approved contractors, and members could use the site to submit a rebate application and supporting documents as well as track the status of rebates.

"Rebates are a unique benefit of being a GVEC member," said General Manager Darren Schauer of the newly introduced rebate website. "Now, it's even easier to take part in this worthwhile program to save both money and energy for the future."[119]

Community Service: A Traditional Member Service

GVEC and its member-owners have long supported the community and youth through a variety of programs dating back to the 1940s. GVEC has continued that focus in the twenty-first century through a vast array of member services including sponsorships, donations, port-a-cool fans for community events, scholarships for higher education, the Power House Energy Investigation program, civic club presentations and participation, Chamber of Commerce support, local parades and festivals, and community trade fairs. Staffers bring Louie the Lightning Bug, Power Town, and the Arcing demonstration to area classrooms to encourage safety, and the GVEC Youth Tour sends emerging young leaders among high school students to Washington, D.C., for a week each year.

Introduced to the membership in 2011, the POWER UP program is made possible through the generous monthly donations of GVEC members. Bills are rounded to the nearest dollar and the difference is donated to the fund which supports financial assistance for electric bills and grants for local nonprofit community projects.

In 2011, GVEC members came together to make an even more meaningful community commitment. The creation of the POWER UP Community fund that year allowed member-owners to round up their monthly electric bills to the nearest dollar and donate the extra change to the charitable fund. In 2012, the first distribution of grants resulted in more than $290,000 donated to community improvement grants as well as electric bill-pay assistance to elderly and low-income GVEC members. Since then, POWER UP funds have been used to purchase new equipment for emergency responders, enhance local health services, and renovate community meeting places among other projects.[120] By the end of 2013, more than $329,000 in community grants were distributed all due to the generous donations of participating GVEC members.

Value in Economic Development: SMI and Motorola

Another type of community service the Cooperative has been involved with over the years is economic development. As long ago as the 1920s, electric utility executives understood that the health of the local utility was tied to the economic vitality of the region it served and Doyle Hines was a tireless promoter of GVEC and the region it called home. For most rural electric cooperatives, the impetus for economic development in their service territories was typically agricultural in nature. And since its formation, GVEC has worked closely with farmers in the area, acquainting them with the latest devices and techniques to make cotton farming, cattle raising, and poultry operations more efficient and productive.

But GVEC also realized early on that a diversified agricultural and industrial economy will provide the jobs and growth necessary to strengthen the service. That realization dates back to 1947 when a native New Yorker had the idea of building a steel mill outside Seguin.

Marvin Selig, who founded SMI (later to become CMC-Texas) in Seguin in 1947, was initially a minor player in the minimill industry because of a lack of capital.

Construction on a new substation dedicated solely to the operations of Seguin's steel mill, Structural Metals Incorporated (SMI), was in process in April 1975.

SMI has grown over the years into CMC Steel Texas as it stands today. The mill has exponentially expanded its operations since the 1970s and remains one of GVEC's largest industrial members and supporters.

In Texas, Structural Metals, Inc., pioneered its first electric arc furnace in 1963. Started as a merchant bar manufacturer in 1947, SMI built its first facility on a one-and-a-half-acre plot near Seguin, Texas, just outside San Antonio. The company would eventually become part of the CMC Steel Group, a $3 billion division of CMC producing more than 3 million tons of steel a year, with downstream operations in rebar and structural fabricating, joist manufacturing and construction.

Clyde Selig, Marvin Selig's younger brother, recalled that SMI's first electric arc furnace, what SMI called the A Furnace, drew prodigious amounts of electric energy from the firm's power suppliers, GVEC and the Lower Colorado River Authority (LCRA).

The mill had a five-thousand-kVa unit, and the electrode busses had to be physically clamped to the transformers. That first furnace operated in a two-vessel configuration.

"When we first struck the arc on A Furnace in 1963," Selig said, "we dimmed the lights from here to Austin."[121]

There is no better example of GVEC's commitment to the economy of the Guadalupe Valley than the leadership role the Cooperative took in enticing a Fortune 500 manufacturer to Seguin in the early 1970s. What became Motorola Corporation's Automotive and Industrial Electronics Group plant in Seguin has produced electronic controls and instrumentation for the automotive and heavy vehicle marketplace since the facility first started up in 1974. But when the huge plant first started investigating Seguin, prospects of it locating in Guadalupe County seemed rather thin.

Doyle Hines, who had been named acting general manager of GVEC in 1971, recalled that after showing interest in Seguin, Motorola backed off. When he got involved in 1972, the plant was not going to be built in Seguin. Hines helped organize a visit of Seguin officials to Motorola's corporate headquarters in La Grange, Illinois, a Chicago suburb.

GVEC General Manager Doyle Hines was directly responsible for Motorola establishing its Seguin assembly plant. The company became a major employer for the area and quickly announced an expansion soon after opening in 1975.

The Motorola Automotive Group was bought by the German company Continental AG in 2006. Continental remains a major employer in the Guadalupe Valley today.

Motorola told the Seguin civic group that it wouldn't build in the community unless it had city water. Hines, who never met a problem he couldn't solve, told Motorola that Seguin would provide access to the city water. Later, in his hotel room, Seguin's Mayor told Hines that the city didn't have the money to run water to the proposed plant.

"We'll furnish the money," Hines said.[122] The mayor asked how. Hines explained that GVEC paid the City of Seguin a franchise tax; the city could pay the Cooperative back by accepting lower tax payments for a number of years.

With a water supply assured, Motorola broke ground for its new plant in 1974 and announced a three-hundred-thousand-square-foot expansion the next year.[123] "The Motorola Plant was a game changer," Hines noted, adding that the new facility employed nearly two thousand people through much of the remainder of the 1970s, 1980s, and 1990s. Even after the Motorola Automotive Group was acquired by Germany's Continental AG in 2006, the Seguin plant continued to employ more than one thousand people producing high-tech automotive electronics components.

GVEC General Manager Darren Schauer (middle) and then Management Assistant Gary Coke (right) celebrate the ground breaking of the Seguin Caterpillar plant alongside Texas Governor Rick Perry (left) in 2009.

The successful siting of the Motorola plant, coupled with an expansion of Randolph Air Force Base, drove the rapidly growing economy of the western end of the territory. In economic development, success drives further success, and the communities of Seguin, La Vernia, and Schertz enjoyed a three-decade-long record of sustained industrial development. SMI continued its expansion and other industries have proudly joined Motorola in siting facilities in the area.

In fact, the combined efforts of GVEC, municipal, county, and state economic development agencies paid dividends in March 2009 when Caterpillar announced it would be building a global assembly, test, and paint facility in Seguin. The new facility

brought with it more than fourteen hundred direct jobs to the area, coupled with capital investment of $170 million. Economic development planners projected an additional twenty-five hundred jobs at primary and secondary suppliers located within thirty miles of Seguin.

In addition to helping attract new business and industry, GVEC has expanded its economic development services over the years to assist local governments with planning and development, providing statistics and demographics, helping to fund recruitment trips and trade fairs, and establishing key relationships with area economic development contacts. Staff also works to cultivate local industrial parks including the DeWitt Industrial Park in Cuero and Cibolo Industrial Business Park off of IH-10 West currently in progress. When completed, the Cibolo Park will attract business to the Cibolo area and also be instrumental in encouraging additional developments in the Schertz and Marion areas. GVEC has assisted with infrastructure needs, as well as offering spec buildings and shovel-ready sites to businesses interested in locating in the service area through developments such as this.[124]

What started as a simple strategy to spur business for GVEC has turned into a respectable service offered by the Cooperative that has helped many organizations receive the resources they critically need to establish operations within GVEC's service area. Darren Schauer explained that GVEC has always focused on the needs and wants of the membership, helping to support their communities, which in the end helps support the members.[125]

Communicating in the Twenty-first Century

By 2013, GVEC was tasked with building a lasting bond with members that now spans over five generations. Communications and public relations in the first seventy years included the introduction of many new member and community services from the Cooperative. That tradition continues today, however going electronic and revitalizing the brand to reach the new generation member is driving member service through communications in the twenty-first century.

Beginning in 2009, the Communications and Public Relations Department was tasked with cobranding GVEC with its subsidiary companies of GVEC.net and GVEC Home Services. Driven by General Manager Darren Schauer, the idea was for members to identify electricity, home services, and Internet with the recognized GVEC name.

The transformation involved the launch of a redesigned www.gvec.org website in 2010, the creation of an application for a mobile website that same year, and the introduction of new GVEC and subsidiary logos in 2011, grouped together under the tagline, "Your kind of power." Communications

and Public Relations conducted member surveys beginning in 2010 to gain feedback on all the changes; member surveys have been conducted biannually since then to gauge awareness levels.

Since 2011, GVEC has slowly been introducing a social media presence to the membership as a way to reinforce a positive image for the Cooperative's brand and provide an additional channel to message members in emergencies and other specific situations. To date, GVEC is communicating with members on Facebook and Twitter.

It Takes an Army to Provide Member Services

Aside from the Member Services Division, other departments in the Cooperative also work hard to make sure that members are served in the best possible ways. What started with primarily directors and linemen has evolved into a virtual army of over 260 employees working in some form or fashion to serve the needs of the GVEC member-owners and its subsidiary customers. As of 2013, needs were being served with pride and passion through the twenty-two areas of Commercial and Industrial Accounts, Member Services, Facilities, Corporate Communications and Public Relations, Economic Development, Operations, Engineering, Technical Services and Communications, Field Services, Customer Service, Information Services, Finance, Accounting, Human Resources, Purchasing, Inventory, Compliance, Safety and Loss Control, Transportation, and the subsidiaries of GVEC Home, GVEC.net., and the Guadalupe Valley Development Corporation. The twenty-first century Cooperative looks very different from the early days, but its purpose of improving the lives of its members remains the same through its conservation and community driven programs, services, and scope of work.

For the leadership and employees of GVEC, thinking beyond electricity in member services is simply a part of the mission to fulfill the needs of those they serve.

The service of GVEC has grown from directors and linemen to over twenty-two different departments with a hand in meeting the needs of member-owners today. Thinking beyond electricity has become a best practice as GVEC evolves with the new cooperative generation.

The GVEC Home appliance showroom in Seguin was opened in 2009.

Chapter **Seven**

Going Beyond Electricity:
GVEC SUBSIDIARY SERVICES

Though members were enjoying an easier lifestyle due to the benefits of electricity, rural areas were lacking other modern conveniences easily accessed by urban communities. To help fill these voids, GVEC has set a precedence of obtaining and offering enhanced services aligned with its purpose of improving life in the Guadalupe Valley.

GVEC has always been keenly aware that electric power isn't the only utility service that rural residents have struggled to obtain. In the Cooperative's earliest days, it signed agreements with Southwestern Bell Telephone Company, General Telephone Company, and Guadalupe Valley Telephone Cooperative allowing the local telephone providers to use its poles to help reduce the expense of bringing telephone service to farms and rural residents. By the early 1960s, telephone companies had strung wire on more than three thousand GVEC poles in the service territory.[126]

The advent of cable television in the 1970s created a similar situation to the advent of electric power in the early twentieth century. Though it was common to receive regular programming across the service territory with an antenna, members in the Western cities such as Seguin and Schertz had access to specialized cable programming. However, similar to the late 1930s, rural members did not.

Co-axial cable, which offered viewers network affiliates and a wider variety of programming, made possible a revolution in television viewing. Customers could receive hundreds of channels of programming, including premium movie channels. Later, cable was used to offer customers pay-television channels, which broadcasted first-run movies.

The only problem was that, like electric power in the early days, cable television depended on population density to make a profit. The farther one was from the center of population, the less likely he or she would

have access to cable. That began changing in the early 1980s when commercial satellites could beam television signals to ten-foot dishes on earth.

By March 1988, GVEC had formed Guadalupe Valley Satellite Communications (GVSC), a division of Guadalupe Valley Development Corporation, to provide its members with rural television. Programming was provided by a newly formed TV cooperative called the National Rural Telecommunications Cooperative of which GVEC

Guadalupe Valley Satellite Communications (GVSC) was established in 1988 and offered satellite television programming to its rural members across the service area. General Manager Doyle Hines felt the service fulfilled a need in the rural areas and fit with the Cooperative's goal to make life better for its members; a philosophy followed still today in regards to subsidiary services.

was a member. General Manager Doyle Hines noted the establishment of GVSC was motivated by the Cooperative's goal of making life better for its members. "Cable television is another service that must be provided if we want to entice new growth into our rural areas," he said.[127]

The Cooperative charged members $2,675 to install the large dish and descramblers for the cable system.[128] Initially, the system offered twelve descrambled channels. In 1989, GVSC was discontinued as technology and miniaturization was coming into play.

By the 1990s, the big dishes were being replaced by smaller dishes about eighteen inches in diamater. Though the technology was changing, rural television still made sense from a Cooperative business perspective because it was a quality of life issue for members in GVEC's service territory. In response, GVEC Rural TV was formed and a franchise to offer the service in the five-county area of DeWitt, Gonzales, Lavaca, Guadalupe, and Wilson was purchased for $500,000. Customers were charged $1,000 to install the small dishes, and by the mid-1990s, more than three thousand members were customers of the Cooperative's rural television service.[129]

In 1997, GVEC sold the business to Golden Sky Systems, Inc., in the amount of $5 million and the profits were reinvested to establish GVEC Home, a subsidiary company that exists today.[130]

GVEC's response to the problem of limited access to television in rural areas of its service territory was typical of the Cooperative's entire approach to member services. If it was a service that members didn't have access to and wanted, then the Cooperative would figure out how to provide it. GVEC would have ample opportunity to demonstrate that same approach during the 1990s and into the twenty-first century.

GVEC.net: Rural Internet Service Provider

From the very beginning, GVEC has been all about meeting the needs of members and providing services to better enjoy life in a rural setting. So when the Internet began to connect the world in the mid-1990s, GVEC didn't hesitate to get deeply involved.

The computer and the broadband Internet service that supports it have revolutionized twenty-first century society. In South Central Texas, these indispensable tools have been made possible by GVEC.net, the Cooperative's business subsidiary that has brought the Internet to rural areas other providers couldn't or wouldn't serve.

In the 1990s, as the large satellite technology scaled down into smaller eighteen-inch dishes, GVSC was discontinued and GVEC Rural TV was formed. It would serve customers through 1997, then be sold to establish GVEC Home Services.

Since the early 1980s, GVEC had been operating an internal communications system utilizing microwave tower links between the Cooperative's offices and substations. GVEC was essentially in the communications business because it had to be from a utility perspective. When the Internet began to manifest itself in the 1990s, GVEC began communicating internally on the worldwide web. At first, the connections were through Internet dial-up modems, and later GVEC was able to get on the Internet through a wireless broadband link.

Darren Schauer, then serving as GVEC General Manager Marcus Pridgeon's assistant, was named manager of the newly formed Computer Information Services Division in 1997. The staff and programmers created a Wide-Area Network and high-speed Local Area Networks to handle internal communications, a major infrastructure investment in itself. Schauer and his team realized that GVEC had the technology in place to provide Internet services to local communities.[131] Once again, as with electric power, telephone, water, and television, GVEC had identified a need and moved to fill it.

Rural members complained that they could not find adequate Internet service that offered local access. Companies providing Internet access charged exorbitant long-distance charges for slow and unreliable service. In 1998, GVEC joined DeWitt County Electric Cooperative and Karnes Electric Cooperative in the establishment of GVEC.net, a separate business housed in GVEC's Gonzales offices.[132] Utilizing the existing microwave towers and substations, GVEC.net made reliable Internet service available to rural residents of the area for $19.95 a month.[133] GVEC.net started with 303 customers in 1998, had grown to a customer base of 5,200 ten years later and had over 7,000 customers by 2013. Today, the Internet Service Provider (ISP) continues to grow and is now offered through a network of fifty-seven towers located across a sixteen-county region of South Central Texas.

In 1998, GVEC.net was established initially offering dial-up Internet services, then moving into high-speed wireless technology. Crews and equipment were a welcome sight for customers as GVEC.net was the only Internet service provider in the rural area, and in many locations, remains so today.

Offering high technology, GVEC.net was one of the only ISP's in the market to offer a live person who could help customers on the phone immediately without an electronic menu of confusing choices in the late 1990s. This was a welcome feature in an age where companies running more efficient operations meant greeting customers with an automated system. And when GVEC.net introduced new technology allowing the ISP to increase customers' broadband speeds called Motorola WiMax in April 2010, it did so automatically without increasing monthly bills.[134] This was a testament to the high level of service GVEC.net was willing to provide their rural customers.

From the beginning, GVEC and its partners have worked to upgrade the GVEC.net experience for member-owners. In the summer of 2013, GVEC.net began to bring Fiber to the Home (FTTH) Internet service to the La Vernia community. FTTH involved the installation of fiber optic cables capable of carrying far more bandwidth than copper wire. Data speeds were increased dramatically, allowing the homeowner the ability to speed up surf time on the web, stream high definition movies, download music faster, send and receive photos more quickly, and experience online gaming without interruption.[135]

By November 2013, GVEC.net had installed one-third of the planned ninety miles of fiber optic cable for the FTTH Internet service. Approximately eleven hundred homes were offered the opportunity to connect to the FTTH network in the first phase of what would be a three-phase project.

"This is an exciting moment for GVEC.net," said GVEC General Manager and CEO Darren Schauer.

After thorough surveys, planning and preparation, GVEC.net chose the La Vernia community to introduce Fiber to the Home Internet, the fastest Internet technology available on the market in 2013. The project was led by (middle to right) Fiber Consultant Robert Russell, Senior Executive Manager Ceason Barnick, and Information Technology Manager Tad Vernor (right).

As the only Internet service provider capable of offering up to one gigabit speeds in the area at the end of 2013, GVEC.net had run "Fiber Power," as they promoted it, to eleven hundred homes in select areas of La Vernia. The second of three phases of construction to ultimately root a ninety-mile planned fiber network was officially in process.

"It was only last May when the Board of Directors of GVEC.net authorized the staff to move forward with this pilot project. We followed through on our commitment to the La Vernia community, and residents can now enjoy the higher speeds of fiber technology in their homes and businesses."[136]

Scheduled for completion in April 2014, the second phase of FTTH Internet service, would offer even more residents in additional La Vernia subdivisions access to the fastest broadband speeds in the industry—up to 1 Gbps.

In its fifteen years of existence, GVEC.net has brought the world to residents of rural South Central Texas. High-speed wireless broadband service has replaced the old dial-up service, and rural members are as well connected to the Web as their city cousins in San Antonio or Houston. Mike Absher, manager of

GVEC's Member Services Division, is a GVEC.net customer himself. Absher lives fourteen miles east of Gonzales, and the only Internet Service Provider he has ever had at his home is GVEC.net.[137] He wouldn't, and couldn't, have it any other way.

GVEC Home: Appliances, AC and Heating, and Renewable Alternatives

In 1998, GVEC made another major decision that would make life easier and more convenient for its members. In June of that year, the Cooperative expanded the thirty-year-old GVEC Appliance Service Shop to offer a broader range of services. The newly created GVEC Home Services, Inc., with offices on Saint Louis Street in Gonzales, offered sales and service of heating and cooling systems, water heaters, and major-brand home appliances.[138]

GVEC Home Services, Inc., which would become GVEC Home in 2009, was opened in Gonzales in 1998. Open to the public, the store was run by Manager Judy Weston under the direction of Member Services Manager Mike Absher and provided residents with a local option for appliances, water heaters, and air conditioning and heating sales and service; the largest contributors to monthly electric use.

Like GVEC.net, GVEC Home Services, Inc., was a stand-alone business that would have to show a profit to justify its existence. GVEC did not enter the ultracompetitive world of appliance sales lightly. In the 1950s and 1960s, the Cooperative had been hesitant about entering into competition with small-town businesses that sold appliances. But by the 1990s, many of those small-town appliance businesses had been supplanted by big-box appliance stores in the cities and suburbs. Rural residents had to drive to the nearest Lowe's or Home Depot in San Antonio or Austin to purchase major appliances and then pay exorbitant delivery charges to have them installed in their homes.

In October 2005, GVEC Home Services opened a second showroom located in La Vernia. By that time, the subsidiary was offering a large selection of energy-efficient brand name home appliances, including Whirlpool, KitchenAid, Estate, GE, Hotpoint, and Friedrich and Rheem. GVEC Home offered member-owners the same service conveniences city residents were able to avail themselves of. In 2009, the subsidiary was rebranded as GVEC Home to encompass its full line of products and services and opened its third and largest showroom to date in Seguin. Adding to its array of services, GVEC Home began offering the Comfort Check program, a two-time per year maintenance program for HVAC systems, which became one of the more popular programs offered by the company.

With a service territory 140 miles across from east to west, GVEC's average appliance service and repair call was 40 to 60 miles. GVEC knew it could compete with the big-box retailers by offering to service

The second GVEC Home Services location would be included in the La Vernia Customer Service Office when it opened in October 2005. Office Manager Paula Kennedy and team would proudly present major appliance brands such as Maytag, Whirlpool, and KitchenAid to shoppers when they would pay a visit and explain how the products and services would help them save money on their electric bills.

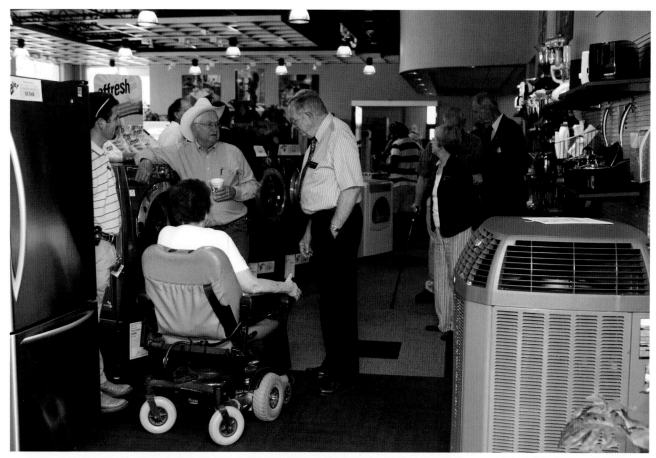

The third and largest GVEC Home showroom to date was opened in Seguin in April 2009. By then the subsidiary had added wind turbines to its product offering to meet the growing interest in renewable alternatives from GVEC members.

GVEC Home introduced its Comfort Check Maintenance Program as a service to help customers maintain the highest energy user in any home; the ac and heating unit. Members had the added benefit of being able to pay the monthly fee for the service on their GVEC electric bill.

Put a New Spin on Your Electric Costs!

Find out how at the New Braunfels Business Trade Show or at any GVEC Home store!

washers, dryers, stoves, refrigerators, and any other major appliances residents might want. Member Services Manager Mike Absher explained that the decision to form GVEC Home also was rooted in the Cooperative's continuing focus on energy efficiency. By selling and servicing heating and cooling systems and major appliances, GVEC can promote the most energy efficient products on the market at any given time. GVEC conducts aggressive marketing campaigns through GVEC Home to make residents aware of the benefits of purchasing and installing top of the line energy efficient products.

"Energy efficiency has always been a big driver for GVEC Home," Absher said.[139]

GVEC Home has also allowed the Cooperative to work with its member-owners on the installation of renewable energy systems. In January 2009, GVEC installed a 1.8-kW Skystream wind turbine at its customer service center under construction in Seguin as a research and educational tool. At the same time, the Cooperative adopted a revised tariff to support the installation of wind turbines at area homes and businesses. GVEC installed a second wind turbine at the Texas Agricultural Education and Heritage Center in Seguin.

GVEC implemented a 1.8 kW wind turbine into the design of its Seguin customer service office in 2009 as a research tool for the Cooperative and an educational tool for the public due to peaking interest in distributive generation (generating power on your own).

The installation of the two wind turbines was important for the future of renewable energy at GVEC, explained General Manager and CEO Darren Schauer. "We need to pinpoint how much electricity these units can realistically generate in our part of Texas in order to determine a true payback scenario for our interested members," Schauer said. "We also want members to see an actual unit in place, see how it looks next to a building, hear how it sounds, etc.—give them some realistic information to base their decision on. We're excited to roll these turbines out for the benefit of our members, the public, and educational purposes."[140]

In July 2009, GVEC Home expanded its footprint in wind energy when it partnered with Southwest Wind Power of Flagstaff, Arizona, and Ontario-based ReDriven Power, Inc., to become an authorized distributor of wind turbines.

Darren Schauer noted that GVEC Home recognized that a certain number of its members wished "to invest in a turbine realizing the existing uncertainties in the technology. We support their energy-conscious efforts and want them to feel comfortable in purchasing from a reliable source such as GVEC Home."[141] After a few years of sales and working more with the technology, GVEC recognized wind turbines were not as effective in South Texas as other areas and with the major manufacturer going out of business and spare parts not easily obtained, GVEC Home ceased sales of wind turbines in 2012.

Still wanting to give customers choices in renewable options, GVEC Home became a distributor for photovoltaic (PV) solar panels. The Cooperative noted that with more than three hundred days of sunshine in the area, most member-owners were attracted to the idea of producing their own electricity and having lower energy bills. GVEC reminded members to have a complimentary energy audit before purchasing a PV solar panel system to ensure maximum efficiency, and helped coordinate each aspect of the sale with well-known area contractors. Solar sales continued to grow for GVEC Home throughout 2013.

In 2012, GVEC Home became a distributor of solar panels in response to inquiries from GVEC members. Solar technology has proved to be a much more viable option for members and continues to be implemented across the service area.

Guadalupe Valley Development Corporation (GVDC): Developed to Meet Rural Water Supply Needs

GVEC's history has always been all about bettering the lives of its consumer members. As early as the late 1980s, GVEC had fully realized that its mandate extended far beyond supplying electric power if it was going to continue to experience growth. That was reflected in the Cooperative's decision to establish the Guadalupe Valley Development Corporation (GVDC) to help meet rural water supply needs. The GVDC would work both for the further development of the region's poultry industry, and later for volunteer fire departments in the GVEC service territory. Eventually, the GVDC would spearhead economic development in the region, helping to attract business and industry into the service area.

As far back as the 1940s, the GVEC service region has supported a vibrant poultry industry and GVEC has long encouraged its members to use electric power wisely and efficiently in poultry operations.

So when officials of Ralston Purina approached General Manager Doyle Hines in the early 1970s about the difficulty of formulating feed with Gonzales County water, Hines listened. The problem was the salt and sulfur in the Gonzales water supply, and Hines knew GVEC had to take action if it wanted to solve the problem for its members who were in the poultry business.[142]

Hines sought Board approval to contact the Farmer's Home Administration offices in Temple, Texas, to urge formation of FHA Rural Water systems in Guadalupe and Gonzales Counties. Eventually, GVEC helped finance East Central Water Supply

Corporation, Springs Hill Water Supply Corporation, Gonzales County Water Supply Corporation, SS Water Supply Corporation, and Green Valley Water Supply Corporation.[143]

Rural water users in the region were able to avail themselves of treatment plants that eliminated much of the salt and sulfur from the local aquifer. The development of the water system also helped create a reliable supply for the numerous volunteer fire departments in the service area. By the late 1990s, the five rural water systems GVEC had helped establish were able to refinance their loans at a much lower interest rate, thanks to financial backing from the Guadalupe Valley Development Corporation.[144]

Once again, GVEC had helped make a difference for rural members in South Central Texas. For the Cooperative, it was business as usual.

Today, the GVDC remains active and plays a part in helping to financially support the economic development goals of the Cooperative by investing in area industrial parks through acquiring land, developing spec buildings and supporting infrastructure to incentivize local development.

To help the rural areas of the Guadalupe Valley continue to develop, the Guadalupe Valley Development Corporation (GVDC) was established in 1989. The GVDC provided loans to bring infrastructure such as water into the service area to help attract new business and industry for growth. The Gonzales County Water Supply Corporation was among the many organizations who got their start due to the financial aid of this GVEC subsidiary.

As of 2013, General Manager Darren Schauer was leading GVEC into an era where electric service has turned from an appreciation to an expectation. He recognizes the challenge of today is to connect to the new generation through providing valuable, relevant services that reach beyond electricity. In doing so, GVEC will fulfill its member promise to be "your kind of power."

Chapter Eight

GVEC Today and TOMORROW

GVEC has developed into a significant part of life in the Guadalupe Valley. Long ago, Cooperative leadership recognized there were more ways than one to light up communities. It is a philosophy that still exists in the work of GVEC today and one that the Cooperative will work to keep relevant for new cooperative generations well into the future.

Three-quarters-of-a-century after local residents cooperated to bring electric power to the farms and small communities of Gonzales and surrounding counties, GVEC is serving over seventy thousand meters in thirteen counties of South Central Texas. The Cooperative's service area stretches approximately one hundred miles east to west, and seventy-five miles north to south, a total of about thirty-five hundred square miles of service territory.[145] That territory is served by more than eighty-five hundred miles of distribution lines stretching from the exurbs of San Antonio east and south to some of the most rural areas in the Lone Star State.

As of 2013, GVEC is operating five area offices in Cuero, Gonzales, La Vernia, Schertz, and Seguin, a state-of-the-art Cooperative Control Center in Gonzales, and a brand-new Western Operations Center in Seguin. More than 260 dedicated employees are attending to the needs of the Cooperative's members and subsidiary customers.[146] The eleven-member Board of Directors is made up of diverse business people from all backgrounds, industries, and communities served by GVEC with Lewis Borgfeld serving as Board president, Melvin E. Strey as vice president, and Don Williams as

TOTAL METERS

73,479

64,890

37,435

28,972

1988 1998 2008 2013

YEAR

GVEC has grown from serving 150 meters in 1940 to over 70,000 meters in 2013.

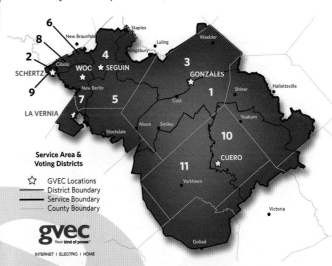

Service Area & Voting Districts

☆ GVEC Locations
— District Boundary
— Service Boundary
— County Boundary

gvec
Your kind of power.®

INTERNET | ELECTRIC | HOME

In 2013, the GVEC service area spans thirty-five hundred miles throughout thirteen counties, primarily in DeWitt, Gonzales, Guadalupe, Lavaca, and Wilson Counties, but also serving parts of Hays, Comal, Fayette, Caldwell, Goliad, Karnes, Victoria, and Jackson Counties.

With its headquarters in Gonzales, the Cooperative has four area customer service offices in Cuero, La Vernia, Schertz, and Seguin as well as one Operations Center in Seguin. Customer Service Representatives at each office conduct business for GVEC as well as GVEC.net Internet services. GVEC Home showrooms are located in Gonzales, La Vernia, and Seguin with plans for a Cuero location to open in 2014.

challenge before them is not just ensuring check marks are made on plan goals, but more so that the plan goals reflect both the current and future needs of the GVEC membership. As a cooperative of the twenty-first century, GVEC recognizes one of its biggest challenges has more to do with generations of members as opposed to electric generation.

Remaining Relevant

The generation that grew up without electricity and provided the backbone of the cooperative movement in America for the past seventy-five years is dwindling from the scene.

To the younger people including Generation X, Generation Y, and Millennials, rural electrification for the most part is ancient history. These are generations that have grown up never having known the inconvenience of not having electric power.

"They really don't care about generation, transmission, and distribution issues," explained Darren Schauer. "The new generation of member-owners does not care who provides them their electric power."[151] That means GVEC and cooperatives nationwide are definitely impacted by this generational change.

For Schauer and the cooperative movement as a whole, "the challenge is how to remain relevant. We are always seeking ways to stay connected with this new generation. We talk a lot about loyalty."[152] But loyalty is a two-way street, and GVEC also talks a lot about value. "When they come to see us," Schauer said, "they don't necessarily think about electric power, but more so the value we are providing in the social and business aspects of their communities. For us, relevance is creating other services that allow us to impact their lives, their Internet, their home, and

GVEC utilizes the diverse experience and knowledge of its management team to identify needs and determine long-range goals for the Cooperative and its subsidiaries. It's a process that helps the team build on the Cooperative's heritage, while keeping a watchful eye on technologies and opportunities to enhance future service. Left to right are Barbara Kuck, Sean Alvarez, Justin Locke, and Bobby Christmas.

their jobs. That's what makes GVEC different."[153] And that difference is what makes GVEC as relevant today as it was to their grandparents' three-quarters-of-a-century ago.

With their roots planted firmly in tradition and a progressive eye on the future, the Cooperative has evolved over seventy-five years into delivering much more than just electricity. In 2013, the team of professionals at GVEC is committed to exceeding their members' expectations by identifying and investing in products and services that fulfill the needs of those they serve. Longtime members hopefully recognize that mission as the unique cooperative way of doing business. To the leadership and staff of GVEC today, it is simply standing behind their pledge to provide "your kind of power."

Appendix

The GVEC Board of Directors

The GVEC Board of Directors are member-owners, too, and are elected by the membership to represent them in the business of GVEC. In the beginning, the Board was primarily made up of local farmers and over the years has grown to include members from diverse backgrounds and industries. Once elected, each director serves for a term of three years (with no limits on terms) and is required to spend time learning all they can about the electric industry to stay current with its many regulations and financial aspects. The Board is also responsible for ensuring cooperative business is handled in accordance with the Bylaws, that financial stability is maintained, and that GVEC's charge of reliability and affordability is achieved. In the last twenty-five years, Board directors who have served the members of GVEC include:

J. P. Lorenz, Jr.	1961–1997
G. D. Nollkamper	1968–1999
Lewis Borgfeld	1974–Current
Tommy Bozka	1975–2000
Melvin Strey	1977–Current
Millard Harborth	1979–1992
W. A. Lott	1981–2011
David Dennis	1984–2009
Robert A. Young, Jr.	1986–2009
Henry Ewald	1992–2000
Don Williams	*1992–Current
David Warzecha	*1993–Current
James Hastings	1997–2007
Robert Werner	1999–Current
Henry Schmidt, Jr.	2000–Current
Tom DeKunder	2001–Current
Emmett Engelke	2008–Current
Shawn Martinez	2009–Current
Mark Roberts	2009–Current
Morris Harvey	2011–Current

Advisory Directors Following Consolidation of DeWitt Electric Cooperative and GVEC

Tilford Steinmann	*1974–2004
Robert Moore	*2000–2001
Tim Voelkel	*1999–2001
Tracy Metting	*1989–2004
Al Janak	*2000–2004

*Tenure began at DeWitt Electric Cooperative

DISTRICT 1: Robert J. Werner

Robert J. Werner has been serving members in District 1 as a GVEC Board director since 1999. He holds a bachelor of business administration degree in management from Sam Houston State University in Huntsville, and he and his wife own and operate Werner's Restaurant in Shiner.

DISTRICT 2: Lewis Borgfeld *Board President*

Lewis Borgfeld has represented District 2 since 1973 when he was appointed to the Board in an advisory capacity. He was then elected to the Board in 1974; in 1986 he was elected Board president. Borgfeld graduated from Schertz/Cibolo High School (now Samuel Clemens High School) and received a bachelor of science degree in business education from Southwest Texas State College (now Texas State University). After graduation, Borgfeld served four years as a pilot in the U.S. Air Force. He currently works in the banking industry as an officer with Schertz Bank and Trust.

DISTRICT 3: Henry C. Schmidt, Jr.

District 3 is represented by Henry C. Schmidt, Jr., who has served GVEC members since 2000. He graduated from Gonzales High School and holds an associate of applied science degree in business management. Schmidt, along with his brother and mother, is an owner of Schmidt and Sons, Inc., a fuel and lubricants distributer. He is also an owner in Apache Express Care and Hesco Maintenance Company, and raises registered Brangus cattle with his wife and son on their ranch in northeast Gonzales County. Schmidt has also served his community as a Gonzales Volunteer Fire Department firefighter and a Gonzales County reserve deputy sheriff.

DISTRICT 4: Shawn Martinez

Shawn Martinez, the representative for District 4, has served on the Board since 2009 and is also the first female Board member of GVEC. She has been in the banking industry since 1995 and currently is vice president loan officer at First Commercial Bank in Seguin. Shawn is an active member of the community, serving as past chairman of the Seguin Area Chamber of Commerce and a board member of the Zonta Club of Seguin and the Navarro Education Foundation.

DISTRICT 5: Morris Harvey

Morris Harvey has served the members in District 5 since 2011. He graduated from Nixon High School and from Texas A&I University in Kingsville in agriculture education. A lifelong rancher, Harvey is also the owner and manager of Mustang Realty in Nixon, and is a broker, real estate professional inspector, and licensed appraiser. He has served his community as a member of the Nixon Hospital Board, Nixon Chamber of Commerce, and as past director of the Feather Fest.

DISTRICT 6: Emmett Engelke

Emmett Engelke has served the members of District 6 since 2008. He was born and raised in Seguin and graduated from Southwest Texas State College (now Texas State University). He worked as a tax auditor/supervisor with the Texas State Comptroller's Department, retiring after thirty-two years of service. Emmett is an active member of Peace Lutheran Church in New Braunfels where he has served on the Church Council and as treasurer of the congregation.

DISTRICT 7: Melvin E. Strey *Board Vice President*

Melvin E. Strey has served District 7 since 1977 and was elected Board vice president in 1992. He was a high school mathematics teacher in the Schertz-Cibolo-Universal City (SCUC) ISD from 1959 to 1989, and owner of Strey Insurance Agency in La Vernia from 1989 to 2007. In addition to his responsibilities on the GVEC Board, Strey is also president of the Board of Directors of East Central Special Utility District and former president of Canyon Regional Water Authority. In his community, he is active in the New Berlin Volunteer Fire Department and the New Berlin Community Club. Although officially retired, Director Strey is still involved with raising cattle along with associated hay and grazing activities.

DISTRICT 8: Mark Roberts

Mark Roberts of District 8 has been a Board director since November 2009. He grew up in Schertz and graduated from Samuel Clemens High School. He received an associate degree of applied sciences from Texas A&M Engineering Extension Service in San Antonio and an accredited automotive management degree from the Automotive Management Institute (AMI) in Bedford, Texas. Roberts owns multiple businesses in Schertz, including Auto Collision Works, Schertz Auto Service Inc., and Roberts Properties, Inc. He is an active member of the community and has served as a volunteer for many causes in and around the City of Schertz.

DISTRICT 9: Tom DeKunder

Dr. Tom DeKunder of Schertz has represented District 9 on the GVEC Board since 2001. He received both his bachelor's and master's degrees in education from Southwest Texas State University (now Texas State University), and earned his doctorate in educational administration from Texas A&M University in College Station. He started his career in teaching in 1968 at O'Henry Junior High in the Schertz-Cibolo-Universal City (SCUC) ISD. He retired from the Marion ISD in 2000 where he served as a teacher, coach, athletic director, campus principal, and district superintendent over a period of thirty years. Dr. DeKunder completed his career in education in 2013 after forty-five years serving as an assistant visiting professor in the Graduate Education Department at St. Mary's University in San Antonio.

DISTRICT 10: Don Williams *Secretary/Treasurer*

District 10 is represented by Don Williams who has served as a Board director since 1992; he was elected secretary/treasurer in 2009. He also serves on the Finance Committee at the First United Methodist Church. Williams previously served nine years as a director of DeWitt Electric Cooperative, two of those years were as Board president. Don is a graduate of Yoakum High School and holds a bachelor of science degree in education and business from Southwest Texas State University (now Texas State University). He is retired from Hochheim Prairie Insurance and is currently a partner with Jacobs-Weber Insurance in Yoakum.

DISTRICT 11: David Warzecha

David Warzecha, representing District 11, has served as a GVEC Board director since 1993. Previously he served as a director for DeWitt Electric Cooperative for eight years and held the office of secretary/treasurer. A businessman and rancher, Warzecha has lived in Dewitt County for more than sixty years. He attended Lindenau and Westhoff schools, graduated from Cuero High School, attended Texas A&M University, and received an associate degree from Victoria College.

Endnotes

1. Videotape Oral History Interview with Noah "Buster" Lindeman, Gonzales, Texas, January 9, 2013.

2. Ibid.

3. Videotape Oral History Interview with Carol DuBose, Gonzales, Texas, January 9. 2013.

4. Allen H. Chessher, *Let There Be Light: A History of Guadalupe Valley Electric Cooperative, 25th Anniversary* (San Antonio: The Naylor Company, 1964), p. 22.

5. Ibid., p. 23.

6. Ibid.

7. Noel "Buster" Lindemann Interview.

8. Ibid., p. 51.

9. Chessher, *Let There Be Light,* p. 52.

10. Robert Caro, *The Path to Power: The Years of Lyndon Johnson*, v. 1 (New York: Vintage Books, 1990), pp. 502-516.

11. Videotape Oral History Interview with Robert Meischen, Yorktown, Texas, January 11, 2013.

12. Ibid.

13. Ibid.

14. Ibid.

15. Ibid. pp. 29-30.

16. Noah "Buster" Lindemann Interview.

17. Chessher, *Let There Be Light,* p. 30.

18. Noah "Buster" Lindemann Interview.

19. Chessher, *Let There Be Light,* p. 31.

20. Ibid.

21. Carol DuBose Interview.

22. Chessher, *Let There Be Light,* p. 37.

23. Ibid.

24. John Williams, "The Story of the Lower Colorado River Authority: A 50th Anniversary Retrospective," 1984, p. 5.

25. Ibid.

26. "Balancing power capacity and customers," *LCRA News,* September 15, 1988, p. 8.

27. "Guadalupe Valley Electric Cooperative marking anniversary in December," *LCRA News,* October 20, 1988, p. 10; See also, "DeWitt County Electric Coop a boon for agriculture for 50 years," *LCRA News,* August 15, 1988, p. 10.

28. Chessher, *Let There Be Light,* p. 33.

29. Ibid.

30. "Schauer Served as President During Crucial Years," *The GVEC Review,* n.d., 1986.

31. Videotape Oral History Interview with Lewis Borgfeld, Seguin, Texas, January 11, 2013.

32. Digitally Recorded Oral History Interview with Darren Schauer, Seguin, Texas, January 13, 2013.

33. "Monroe Schauer," *The Victoria Advocate,* May 8, 1990.

34. Lewis Borgfeld Interview.

35. Ibid.

36. Ibid.

37. O. W. Davis, "A Farewell Message," *GVEC Information Bulletin,* January 1972, p. 1.

38. "Hines Succeeds Davis as Gen. Mgr.," op. cit.

39. "General Manager Hines Set To Retire in December," *GVEC Review,* November 1993.

40. Digitally Recorded Oral History Interview with Robert Young, Seguin, Texas, January 10, 2013.

41. Ibid.

42. Videotape Oral History Interview with Marcus Pridgeon, Gonzales, Texas, January 11, 2013.

43. Darren Schauer Interview.

44. Ibid.

45. Williams, "The Story of the Lower Colorado River Authority: A 50th Anniversary Retrospective," p. 9.

46. Ibid., p. 10.

47. Marcus Pridgeon Interview.

48. Ibid.

49. Darren Schauer Interview.

50. Ibid.

51. Ibid.

52. "President's and General Manager's Message," *2010 GVEC Annual Report,* p. 3.

53. Darren Schauer Interview.

54. "President's and General Manager's Message," *2010 GVEC Annual Report,* p. 3.

55. Darren Schauer, "Strategic Wholesale Power Decision Made," *The GVEC Review,* January 2011, p. 17.

56. "GVEC Receives 'A+' Rating from Standard & Poor's," *The GVEC Review,* January 2007, p. 1.

57. "GVEC Earns Top Credit Ratings from Fitch," GVEC Press Release, April 5, 2010, p. 1.

58. Ibid.

59. Ibid.

60. O. W. Davis, "Manager's Comments," *Co-op News and Views,* May 1954, p. 2.

61. "Here's New Seguin District Office," *Information Bulletin,* June 1956, p. 1.

62. "REA Approves Application For New Loan of $1,145,000," *Information Bulletin,* June 1956, p. 2.

63. Karen Yancy, *And There Was Light: A History of Guadalupe Valley Electric Cooperative* (Fort Worth: Eakin Press, 1989), p. 14.

64. News Item, *The GVEC Review,* January 1980.

65. "Keeping the Lights On," *2002 GVEC Annual Report.*

66. President's and General Manager's Message, *2013 GVEC Annual Report,* p. 13.

67. "Facts About All-Electric Home Rate," Insert, *Information Bulletin,* September 1956.

68. "Year-round Comfort," *Information Bulletin,* March 1958, p. 1.

69. News Item, *The GVEC Review,* May 2005.

70. Marcus Pridgeon Interview.

71. Digitally Recorded Oral History Interview with Jim Springs, Seguin, Texas, January 12, 2013.

72. Ibid.

73. Ibid.

74. Marcus Pridgeon Interview.

75. Darren Schauer Interview.

76. Digitally Recorded Oral History Interview with Gerald Moltz, Seguin, Texas, January 11, 2013.

77. Ibid.

78. Digitally Recorded Oral History Interview with Ronnie Foreman, Seguin, Texas, January 13, 2013.

79. Digitally Recorded Oral History Interview with Bobby Christmas, Seguin, Texas, January 12, 2013.

80. Ibid.

81. Digitally Recorded Oral History Interview with Gary Wilson, Seguin, Texas, January 12, 2013.

82. Bobby Christmas Interview.

83. Ibid.

84. Ibid.

85. Ibid.

86. Ibid.

87. Digitally Recorded Oral History Interview with Betty Leon Netardus, Gonzales, Texas, January 10, 2013.

88. Digitally Recorded Oral History Interview with Betty Nell DuPree, Gonzales, Texas, January 10, 2013.

89. Ibid.

90. Ibid.

91. Ibid.

92. Darren Schauer Interview.

93. Ibid.

94. Digitally Recorded Oral History Interview with Bobby O'Neal, Gonzales, Texas, January 10, 2013.

95. President's and Manager's Message, *1996 GVEC Annual Report,* p. 2.

96. *2001 GVEC Annual Report,* p. 4.

97. Telephone Oral History Interview with Bobby Christmas, Gonzales, Texas, December 8, 2013.

98. *2008 GVEC Annual Report,* p. 5.

99. *2009 GVEC Annual Report,* p. 3.

100. *2010 GVEC Annual Report,* p. 3.

101. Ibid.

102. *Your Co-op Magazine,* v. 1, no. 1, April 1953, p. 1.

103. "Willie Wiredhand Says," *Co-op News and Views,* v. 1, no. 3, June 1953, p. 8.

104. "Electric Brooders Increase Profits," *Information Bulletin*, v. 3, no.9, September 1957, pp. 2–3.

105. "Co-op Employs Power Use Advisor," *Information Bulletin*, v. 4, no. 11, November 1958, p. 1; See Also, "News Item," *Information Bulletin*, v. 3, no. 9, September 1957, p. 2.

106. "News Item," *Information Bulletin*, v. 3, no. 9, September 1957, p. 2.

107. Chessher, *Let There Be Light*, p. 87.

108. Yancy, *And There Was Light*, p. 22.

109. "GVEC Installs 10,000th Load Control Device," *The GVEC Review*, October 1990, p. 1.

110. "Ask an Energy Expert," *The GVEC Review*, June 2008, p. 6.

111. "Free Home Energy Audit," http://www.gvec.org/yeFreeHomeEnergyAudit.aspx

112. Ibid.

113. "GVEC Uses Camera to Help Solve Homeowner's Energy Efficiency Problems—Thermal Images Provide Colorful Clues," GVEC Press Release, February 23, 2012.

114. "Texas Energy Codes," *The GVEC Review*, February 2007, p. 6.

115. "Conservation Plan 7," http://www.gvec.org/ycoopConservationPlan7.aspx

116. Ibid.

117. "We've Got the 'Power Tools' to Help," GVEC Brochure, February 2013, p. 2.

118. Ibid.

119. Darren Schauer, "Exciting Developments at GVEC," *The GVEC Review*, February 2011, p. 19.

120. "It's Empowering Communities," *The GVEC Review*, May 2011, p. 23.

121. Clyde Selig Comments to the Author, January 15, 2010, p. 3.

122. Doyle Hines Interview.

123. *Motorola Corporation 1975 Annual Report*, pp. 14–15.

124. *2010 GVEC Annual Report*, p. 10.

125. Darren Schauer Interview.

126. Chessher, *Let There Be Light*, p. 87.

127. Milton D. Hines, "Manager's Report," *The GVEC Review*, June 1990, p. 3.

128. "Rural TV Service Program Announced," *The GVEC Review*, May 1988, p. 6.

129. Digitally Recorded Oral History Interview of Mike Absher, Gonzales, Texas, January 9, 2013.

130. Ibid.

131. Darren Schauer Interview.

132. "GVEC.net," *1998 GVEC Annual Report*, p. 11.

133. Ibid.

134. *2010 GVEC Annual Report*.

135. *2013 GVEC Annual Report*.

136. President's Message, *2013 GVEC Annual Report*.

137. Mike Absher Interview.

138. "GVEC Home Services," *1998 GVEC Annual Report*, p. 11.

139. Mike Absher Interview.

140. "GVEC Promotes the Use of Renewable Energy," GVEC Press Release, January 30, 2009, p. 2.

141. "GVEC Announces Wind Turbine Dealership Agreement," GVEC Press Release, July 13, 2009, p. 1.

142. Doyle Hines Interview.

143. Yancy, *And There Was Light*, p. 49.

144. Ibid.

145. *2010 GVEC Annual Report*, p. 9.

146. Darren Schauer, "Looking Forward to 2013," *The GVEC Review*, v. 39, no. 1, January 2013, p. 17.

147. "A Message from the President & GM," *2012 GVEC Annual Report*, p. 2.

148. Darren Schauer, "2012 GVEC Business Plan," *The GVEC Review*, January 2012, p. 17.

149. Ibid.

150. Darren Schauer, "Planning Wisely for the Long Term," *The GVEC Review*, September 2012, p. 17.

151. Telephone Oral History Interview with Darren Schauer, Seguin, Texas, April 4, 2014.

152. Ibid.

153. Ibid.

Index

About the Authors

Tammy THOMPSON

Corporate Communications and Public Relations Manager Tammy Thompson began her career with the Guadalupe Valley Electric Cooperative in 2008. Thompson holds a Bachelor of Arts degree in business from Concordia University Texas and has worked as a marketing and communications professional for over twenty-one years. Born and raised in Seguin, Texas, much of her childhood was spent in small rural towns such as Gonzales and Smiley, near to the birthplace of GVEC. Coupled with many years of working and studying in San Antonio and Austin, she feels at home serving the good people and vibrant communities of the Guadalupe Valley. Tammy resides in Seguin, Texas, with her husband of twenty-one years, Gannon, and two sons, Dustin and Kyle.

Thompson humbly shares much of the credit for her first writing with her staff, co-workers, leadership, and co-writer Bill Beck; without whom this historical seventy-five-year journey of GVEC would not have been possible.

"Throughout this project, I have developed the deepest respect for the collective efforts of each and every past and present GVEC Board director, general manager, and employee. Together, we have truly built a cooperative founded upon providing genuine service, doing what's right, and making a positive impact on real lives. What an honor it is to personally share in that accomplishment and to have the opportunity to tell the unique story of GVEC." — Tammy Thompson

Bill BECK

Writer and historian Bill Beck of Lakeside Writers' Group has more than a quarter-century of experience writing about business and institutional history. He wrote his first history for Minnesota Power in 1985, and has more than 130 published books to his credit. He has written anniversary books for Houston Lighting & Power Company and Central Power & Light Company in Corpus Christi. He is currently completing anniversary histories for Donaldson Company in Bloomington, Minnesota, and Acme Brick Company in Fort Worth, Texas.

Beck is a 1971 graduate of Marian University in Indianapolis and did his graduate work in American History at the University of North Dakota. Beck started Lakeside Writers' Group twenty-eight years ago following ten years as a reporter for newspapers in Minnesota and North Carolina and seven years as the senior writer in the Public Affairs Department at Minnesota Power, an electric utility in Duluth. He lives in the Irvington neighborhood of Indianapolis with Elizabeth, his wife of forty-nine years.